PARTS *of* Me
Sylvia Bredenkamp

PARTS *of Me*

Yearning for Revival

Sylvia Bredenkamp

Copyright

Published by:
Sylvia Bredenkamp

Contact
Sylvia Bredenkamp
thegodwhoheal@gmail.com

Edited by
Diane Thompson
di2thomps@gmail.com

DTP
Clive Thompson
International Professional Book Designer
www.getclive.com
email: cliveleet@mweb.co.za
+27 83 761 0698 cell
+27 31 207 4884 studio

Printed by
Pinetown Printers, Durban

ISBN: 978-0-620-66278-9

Scripture Reference

Scripture quotations have been extracted (as considered appropriate) from the following versions of the Holy Bible:

New Living Translation,
Copyright © 1996, 2004, 2007 by Tyndale House Publishers, Wheaton, Illinois 60189
Used by permission.
All rights reserved.

The King James Version,
Copyright © 1982 by Thomas Nelson, Inc.
Used by permission.
All rights reserved.

The Amplified Bible,
Copyright ©1954, 1958, 1962, 1964, 1965, 1987 by The Lockman Foundation (www.Lockman.org).
Used by permission.
All rights reserved.

Complete Jewish Bible
by David H. Stern. Copyright © 1998.
All rights reserved. Used by permission of Messianic Jewish Publishers, 6120 Day Long Lane, Clarksville, MD 21029

Disclaimer

This book must be seen as additional information, amplifying and complementing already published books with similar context.

Although the content of this book contains psychological and medical information, the author has made every effort to use terminology that is understandable for every type of reader. The author is not in conflict with any medical or psychiatric institution or representative, nor with any church and/or religious doctrine.

Together we, as believers in Christ, are all ministers of righteousness and ministers of Jesus the Christ (Romans 13:6, 1 Corinthians 4:1, 2 Corinthians 11:15).

Great effort has been made to make this book as complete and as accurate as possible. However, there may be mistakes in the content.

God exhort us to test and prove everything according to Scripture, so you are welcome to test the facts in this book.

Every effort has been made to trace copyright holders and I apologize in advance for any omissions. I would be pleased to insert the appropriate acknowledgements in any subsequent addition of this publication.

Pseudonyms (pennames) are used in examples and case studies to protect the identities of the actual persons.

The author shall have neither liability nor responsibility to any person or entity with respect to any loss or damage caused or alleged to have been caused directly or indirectly by the information contained in this book.

Caution to the Reader

If you are taking medication for any disease, mental illness or disorder, do NOT make any changes in your medication without seeing your physician or psychiatrist. Withdrawal from medication without competent medical supervision can be extremely hazardous to your health.

The information presented in this book is intended for your knowledge and to give insight into the areas of physical, emotional, mental and spiritual disorders or diseases and their origin and solutions.

Contents

Dedication

My Heavenly Father

I would like to dedicate this book firstly to my Heavenly Father. Thank You, Abba, for Your unmerited mercy, Your sufficient grace, Your unconditional, unfailing, consuming Love, Your daily protection, Your faithfulness and Your magnificent gift of life. Thank You that You daily cleanse me and teach me. I give You all the glory and the honour for what You have done in my life and also for that which is still to come. May Your perfect will be done through this book.

My husband, André

Secondly, I would like to dedicate this book to my husband, André. You have loved me unconditionally and you have laid down your life for me. Together, we have been on this journey chasing revival. And man.... it has been tough, it has been exciting, it has been life-changing and I absolutely love every moment doing it with you. Thank you for being you. Thank you for standing up for me and thank you for being my covering and my pillar. Thank you for being a father to our three precious children. I honour you for the man that you are. I love you with all my heart!

Introduction

Revival – *a word which is heard more and more in conversations amongst believers in Christ.*

Across the world today, there is a growing cry to God for a divine visitation; *for revival.* It is the hearts of people yearning for more... more joy, more peace, more life, more power. There are very few churches in the western world that do not have this hope in their hearts and on their prayer agendas. They are saying that what they are currently experiencing is not enough; that they need a new season of refreshing from the Presence of God. They have heard of times in the past when God visited His people and restored their lives, families and cities. They are excited by the possibility of a fresh Wind of God's Spirit in the Church.

The word 'revival' literally means the following:
- Bringing back to health;
- Recovery;
- Returning to life or consciousness;
- Bringing back into use;
- Activity;
- Reawakening of faith.

With this in mind and when we look at the world around us, we are so desperately in need of revival!

Historically, a revival has been seen as an increase and a renewal of spiritual life in a church or a society. Revivals are seen as the restoration of the Church itself to a vital and fervent relationship with God after a period of moral decline. Mass conversions of non-believers are seen. These movements of the Holy Spirit are often followed by signs, wonders and miracles through which the power of God is put on display.

Since early Church history, names such as Smith Wigglesworth and Kathryn Kuhlman are remembered when the topic of revival pops up. These were great men and woman of God whose hearts were on fire and they were passionate to see the Kingdom of Heaven manifested on earth. These movements of the Holy Spirit manifested in so many different ways and touched smaller groups of people and thousands of people at one given moment.

One man, who I really admire and who is still making a huge impact in people's lives today, is Derek Prince. Derek Prince (1915-2003) was one of the most prominent Bible teachers of the 20th century and his ministry touched millions of people across the world. His books and teachings continue to be a source of inspiration and insight to Christians today. He is well known as one of the founders of the charismatic movement and his wide influence has brought healing, deliverance, empowerment and maturity to countless thousands in every continent.

We are living in a day and age where revival cannot singularly depend on the fire that burns in any one person's heart. We cannot sit and wait for someone to usher in the *Presence of Almighty God* to bring the 'more' we yearn for. We long for refreshment and permanent change in our lives and in our communities.

We know the Great Commission and we pray *"Thy kingdom come, Thy will be done on earth, as it is in heaven"*, yet we hope that someone else will be a Kathryn Kuhlman or a Derek Prince. Revival starts with us – with me and you. It starts when you surrender every part of who you are, or who you think you are, to a loving Heavenly Father; when you allow Him to search out all things which are not part of who

He created you to be; when you allow Him to cleanse every part of your being and set you apart for the very purpose for which He has created you – when you are filled with a greater measure of His Love and of His Spirit.

"May He grant you out of the rich treasury of His glory to be strengthened and reinforced with mighty power in the inner man by the Holy Spirit. May Christ through your faith dwell in your hearts! ...That you may really come to know through experience for yourselves the love of Christ ... that you may be filled through all your being unto all the fullness of God [may have the richest measure of the divine Presence, and become a body wholly filled and flooded with God Himself]" (Ephesians 3:16-19).

Revival is not a once-off event where you are touched by God and have a 'WOW!' experience. Revival is a relationship (continual fellowship) with the only true God. We have misunderstood revival, seeing it as either a church or an evangelistic event or events. Revival, however, cannot be humanly organized because it is a personal intimate meeting with God; receiving a greater measure of Christ's fullness –

"...until we all attain oneness in the faith and in the comprehension of the full and accurate knowledge of the Son of God, that we might arrive at really mature manhood (the completeness of personality which is nothing less than the standard height of Christ's own perfection), the measure of the stature of the fullness of the Christ and the completeness found in Him" (Ephesians 4:13).

"Remain in Me, and I will remain in you" (John 15:4).

"Anyone who eats My flesh and drinks My Blood remains in Me, and I in him" (John 6:56).

"When I am raised to life again, you will know that I am in

My Father, and you are in Me, and I am in you" (John 14:20).

God's heart was never to just visit us, but to abide (dwell) in us – to have intimacy with us. As He dwells in us, we experience His perfect love and acceptance. We were all created for this perfect love. Every part of our being is crying out for love. As you get into a right relationship with Him, you will not only see, but ultimately experience His power being demonstrated in your heart and life. His victorious, resurrection life and His perfect love will fill you and overflow through you to other people. This is revival in its essence. This is the only way in which revival is not only lasting, but also increasing and progressive. In this way, we will not just see one single man or woman initiating revival meetings every once in a while, but rather thousands of believers sharing their overflow in humility and unconditional love – surrendered in obedience to a mighty Heavenly Father.

Unfortunately, the global Church does not always believe this, because her identity and calling are distorted. The Church is looking for revival and transformation, but there is no reformation from the inside out. She does not see herself as the significant, called out one who has to usher in the King of Heaven and His glorious presence. Or, she is deceived and thinks she is doing all the right 'stuff', but she is like the churches in the Book of Revelation which John writes about in Revelation Chapters 2 and 3.

Over the next few chapters of this book, I will be giving you an overview of God's magnificent creation of each one of us, how our blindness and brokenness has affected every part of us in such a way that we are not fulfilling our destiny as revivalists. The Body of Christ, the Church – you, who are reading this book, can be the next great revivalist if you just trust and believe Him above all else.

Ephphatha! – that is Be Opened! (Mark 7:34)

May your ears be opened to what the Spirit of God has to say to you.

I pray that, as you read, the Spirit of God will move and breathe into the whole of your being and give you power and bring complete healing where needed, so that you can be all that He has called you to be – for such a time as this!

PARTS of Me
Yearning for Revival

Chapter 1

Created in His Likeness

"Then God said, Let Us make mankind in Our image, in Our likeness, so that they may rule over the fish in the sea and the birds in the sky, over the livestock and all the wild animals, and over all the creatures that move along the ground. So God created mankind in His own image, in the image of God He created them; male and female He created them" (Genesis 1:26-27).

It was God's desire to create someone like Himself (His character), to whom He could relate and have relationship with and whom He could trust to have dominion, power and authority over the creatures. In the last verse of the above scripture, "created in His image" is repeated for the certainty that it might be taken notice of, as if God is showing man's superior glory and dignity to the rest of the creatures. We were made to be eternal beings like God; truly righteous and holy (Ephesians 4:24), to display the glory of God (1 Corinthians 11:7) and to know who we are in Him (Colossians 3:10,12).

Each and every person is intricately made by God and in God's image – in His likeness.

An image is a person or thing that resembles another closely. In other words, God created us in such a way that we should resemble Him – His nature (character). Seeing that He has made us as an image, He also knows us so well. As people, we are so aware of our image and how the world sees us, yet God gave each one of us his/her own perfect, personally handcrafted image – long before we had an image in the world's eyes.

"And all of us, as with unveiled face, because we continued to behold, as in a mirror, the glory of the Lord, are constantly being transfigured into His very own image in ever- increasing splendour and from one degree of glory to another; for this comes from the Lord Who is the Spirit" (2 Corinthians 3:18).

As in a mirror, we gaze into His eyes and we see His glory. During this experience of intimacy with Him, we are constantly transformed into His likeness – ever-increasing, from one level of glory to another. As His Spirit reveals who He is, we begin to see who we are in Him. We begin to know in a very deep way what we 'look' like. A glance at Jesus captures our hearts (Song of Solomon 4:9) but gazing into His mirror brings transformation and glory.

The 'mirror' of God reflects a perfect image of who we are, but if we lose our focus and we look away for a brief moment, we lose the true reflection. Temptation and deceptive lies come along and we fall for them, just like Eve in the garden. Fear, shame and guilt overwhelm us and we lose intimacy with God. We forget what our true image looks like and, instead of looking up, we begin to look down or around us. We compare ourselves to others and start to live according to perceived, false beliefs and expectations. We become blinded by the god of this world (2 Corinthians 4). God has not gone away, yet we cannot see Him. We look into mirrors that are faulty. I remember, as a child, having been to one of those 'hall of mirrors' on the Durban beachfront with my sister. I found different shapes and sizes of mirrors and some of them really made me look very funny and very distorted. That is exactly what happens when we do not see the clear reflection in God's mirror. We start to have a distorted view of who we are and soon we say things like: "I am stupid"; "I am not as good as she is", "I don't live in that suburb, and therefore I don't feel welcome amongst that group". Even in church, we hear it; "Oh, I am not as spiritual as they are" or "I am not as gifted or prophetic" or "I am not as important as the pastor". Titles, position and the balance of one's bank account become very important to people. Dominion and rule over other people creep in instead of having Godly dominion and rule over creation as God intended.

Something very similar happens when you come to Christ. You were in the world – blinded and seduced by the things of this world. When you accept Christ as Lord and Saviour (you glance at Him), He takes the blindfold off (you are unveiled), but your eyes are so sensitive to the light that you cannot see a clear image yet. Your eyes have to get used to the light and as you begin to see, you see more and learn and understand more until you gaze fully into His mirror and see a beautiful, perfect picture of Him as Father and you as His son/daughter. Sadly, most people come to Christ and lose the blindfold, but they never lose their blinded state because the light of God does not have enough opportunity to expel the darkness which their eyes are still accustomed to. They are still entertained by the things of this world and still have to learn to resist the temptations of sin and what they expose themselves to. You cannot see more light if you continue to expose yourself to darkness. God is Light and in Him there is no darkness.

When children are exposed to neglect, lack or abuse, they grow up with a much-distorted view of themselves and of God. Sometimes people have been in darkness for generations because of the things their parents and forebears were involved in and it means that you constantly must choose to fix your gaze on Him and to allow His light to expel the darkness in your life.

When God gave life to you through your biological parents, He put inside of you gifting and purpose. Your heart's deepest desires, gifting and purpose naturally outwork themselves when you fulfil your God-given destiny, which is part of His plan for creation. If you never discover who you are or what you are supposed to be doing in life, you never fulfil your destiny.

> *"The Lord looks from Heaven, He beholds all the sons of men; From His dwelling place He looks [intently] upon all the inhabitants of the earth – He Who fashions the hearts of them all, Who considers all their doings"* (Psalm 33:13-15).

Each one of us is carrying something of the character of our magnificent Creator inside of us. There is only one you. There is something within you that this world desperately needs. If you are not you, the world misses out on you – and something in God's plan for creation is missing.

Chapter 2

The Tri-Part Being

It is very clear from Scripture that we were created as spiritual beings with a soul and a body.

> "...and may your spirit and soul and body be preserved..." (1 Thessalonians 5:23).
> "...dividing of soul and spirit, of both joints and marrow..." (Hebrews 4:12).

Our Creator has created us as tri-part beings – every part of us, created in love and with great delight – all to reflect His glory and splendour.

> "For You did form my inward parts; my frame was not hidden from You when I was being formed in secret and intricately and curiously wrought [as if embroidered with various colours]" (Psalm 139:13-15).

Therefore, it is so vital to make sure that we tend to each and every part of our being in order to keep us from missing our creative purpose.

> "Do not offer any part of yourself to sin as an instrument of wickedness, but rather offer yourselves to God as those who have been brought from death to life; and offer every part of yourself to Him as an instrument of righteousness" (Romans 6:13).

"Then the LORD God formed a man from the dust of the ground and breathed into his nostrils the breath of life, and the man became a living being" (Genesis 2:7).

With the above scriptures in mind, let us look a bit more deeply into our creative parts and discover how gloriously and magnificently God has woven us together in the womb.

The Body

Our bodies are obviously the physical part of our creation. We were made from the dust of the earth. Interestingly enough, it is a scientific fact that the earth/soil (dust of the earth) is made up of exactly the same nutrients found in our extremely complex bodies.

After conception, the embryo develops into three parts (germ layers) known as the ectoderm, the mesoderm and the endoderm. All the organs of the body develop from one of these three germs layers to make up our entire physical being. In short, this is how it is divided:

The *ectoderm* forms the skin, the eyes, the ears, the nose, nervous system, brain and spinal cord;

The *mesoderm* forms the bone, marrow, muscles, connective tissue, blood cells, heart, kidneys, tongue, blood vessels and the lymph glands;

The *endoderm* forms the respiratory system, the liver, gastro intestinal system, endocrine glands and organs and the urinary system.

Even the human body is made up of three parts, working in unity and harmony to ensure that the spirit and soul of man have a healthy, safe environment through which to express themselves.

The moment we give our lives to Jesus and declare that He alone is Lord and Saviour, God abides in us (in our bodies) through His Spirit, together with our soul and spirit. We are then choosing to give our bodies back to Him, to be Lord over our bodies (our physical health and wellbeing). Making Him Lord over our bodies is the first step and the second step is to take responsibility for our bodies.

The following are the four main ways in which we responsibly care for our bodies –
1. Accept our bodies;
2. Be physically active;
3. Eat and drink wisely;
4. Consecration.

"Don't you realize that your body is the temple of the Holy Spirit, who lives in you and was given to you by God? You do not belong to yourself" (1 Corinthians 6:19).

"...let us cleanse ourselves from everything that contaminates and defiles body and spirit and bring consecration to completeness in the reverential fear of God" (2 Corinthians 7:1).

When we live a life without Jesus, we do what we want with our bodies and the Holy Spirit does not dwell in us. Our bodies are a gift – an amazing creation of God and we should treat it with respect; not making an idol out of it or being obsessed about how we look but making sure that it is well nurtured and in good health.

Accepting Your Body

Many people look in the mirror and are so dissatisfied with their bodies – butt too big; chest too small; nose too pointy; eyes too far apart; big thighs; skinny calves. When God says we are *'fearfully and wonderfully made'* (Psalm 139:14), we do not always get the 'wonderfully made' part. We all want to look 'good' but most of us are convinced that we look 'bad' in one way or another, even if we are satisfied with our overall appearance.

What is a perfect body? Who determines what perfection looks like? In Matthew 5:48, Jesus says, *"Be ye therefore perfect, even as your Father which is in heaven is perfect."* The word 'perfect' means to be complete in various applications of labour, growth, mental and moral character. As Christians, we translate that perfection into every area of our lives and we manage to effectively mask our deficiencies in the other areas. But it is so hard to hide our physical imperfections. With the help of today's medical and surgical interventions, we try hard to live up to a standard of perfection that was set by the spoken words of people around us and by the media in all its forms.

We have fallen into the trap where the inner image of our perfect self falls more in line with how we look on the outside. If you even try to blame God for the devalued worldly beauty and perfection, you are barking up the wrong tree.

In Songs of Solomon, King Solomon expresses his love and passion towards his beautiful 'beloved'. These few chapters in the Bible are often seen as an allegory of God's love for us; and if you have not noticed before, treat yourself by reading how Solomon describes his beloved. She is most definitely not my idea of a physically perfect woman. Yet he is absolutely head-over-heels in love with her.

It is not so much your body that needs to change, but your perception of your body that needs renewing. Instead of fighting against our own perceptions, we need to learn to accept our uniqueness. In order for you to accept and embrace the body God designed, you must break the chains of worldly perceptions about who you are and how valuable you are. It takes courage to accept yourself the way you are right now. Instead of focusing on what you see as imperfect, rather focus on what you can do to make things right. You are not perfect. So, who is perfect on this planet? Even the 'perfect' movie stars have cellulite and wrinkles. Your physical appearance does not determine who you really are.

In 1 Corinthians 6:19 (the abovementioned scripture), we learn that our bodies are a temple of the Holy Spirit. In Exodus, the Creator of the universe takes great care and time to give specific detail on how He wanted the tabernacle (temple) to be built – the colours, the embroidery work, the furniture etc. God wanted His dwelling place to be functional and beautiful – a place where His presence and glory could be displayed. In exactly the same way, God took time to knit us together in our mother's womb (Psalm 139). He tended to the specific detail of our bodies so that each one of us can be a functional, beautiful, movable temple for His Spirit, perfect in His sight; that His will can be carried out in the world.

Be Physically Active

In the beginning, God placed man in the garden, which so happened to be outdoors, not indoors in front of the television set. They had to tend to their garden and work daily. Physical activity makes you sweat and, because you are active, your body remains fit and healthy. Most of us do not like sweat because it is the result of hard work. It is also very smelly and very sticky, so we avoid it. In our modern, technologically advanced society, things are done so easily and without much effort, making physical movement less and less. Physical activity is good for the body and that is no secret.

Here are just a few benefits:
- Stronger muscles and flexibility;
- Lower risk of heart disease;
- Lower blood pressure;
- Helps to control cholesterol;
- Prevents obesity;
- Improves emotional health;

- Stress relief;
- Better sleep;
- Increases metabolism;
- Stronger immune system.

Physical exercise, particularly continuous aerobic exercises such as running, cycling and swimming, has many cognitive benefits and effects on the brain. Influences on the brain include increases in neurotransmitter (chemicals that transmit signals from one nerve cell to another) levels, improved oxygen and nutrient delivery, and increased neurogenesis (the process by which nerve cells are generated) in the hippocampus (part of the brain that is involved in memory forming). The effects of exercise on memory have important implications for improving children's academic performance, maintaining mental abilities in old age, and the prevention and potential cure of neurological diseases.

Does this mean that you must go out tomorrow and run 10km? Of course not! It is vital, however, to find ways in your daily life to increase your physical activity. You can then gradually increase these activities as you become fitter.

Eat and Drink Wisely

From the very beginning, humans have loved food. We can go totally overboard with our choices when it comes to what/how we eat and drink.

What to eat:
Fruit is not only easy to digest, but it adds a vital dimension to our diet with its rich supply of enzymes and organic nutrients. Fruit has a good cleansing effect on the digestive system and is a brilliant source of energy.

Vegetables are the best source of all minerals and provide the vitamins we need for healthy living.

God designed certain foods to grow in different seasons as your body's nutritional needs change with these different seasons. Although many people go the vegetarian way these days, eating meat is very Biblical and very healthy. There is no definite indication as to what man's diet was before the flood. However, after the flood, God clearly instructed that man can eat meat. The only restriction God gave was that the blood was not allowed to be consumed. This includes the very famous black pudding (generally made from pork fat or beef suet and pork blood) consumed in Great Britain, Ireland and in other parts of Europe. Not only are you overstepping a spiritual boundary, but you can defile yourself because animal blood often carries viruses that can cause deadly diseases when eaten. Blood is a special fluid that carries nutrients and oxygen which sustain our lives, as long as we keep our bloodstreams clean and uncontaminated.

> *"Every moving thing that lives shall be food for you; and as I gave you the green vegetables and plants, I give you everything. But you shall not eat flesh with the life of it which is its blood"* (Genesis 9:4).

> *"Just take care not to eat the blood, for the blood is the life, and you are not to eat the life with the meat. Do not eat it, so that things will go well with you and with your children after you, as you do what Adonai (the Lord your God) sees as right"* (Deuteronomy 12:23-25).

In order to have a body that can function well and cope with the stresses of life and infections which we are exposed to, we have to make sure that we have a balanced, nutritious diet. We have to take into consideration that some of our fresh meat, fruit and vegetables are genetically and chemically modified and processed, which means that we do not necessarily get enough nutrition. During the process of being precooked and frozen or processes to prolong shelf life, organic enzymes, vitamins and minerals are destroyed. Try, therefore, to avoid these and rather eat fresh fruit and vegetables. Try to eat raw, fresh and organic foods as much as you possibly can. Grow your own if you can.

Sugar, in its natural form as glucose, is a vital nutrient for the functioning of the brain and body organs. It becomes harmful to the body when refined and processed. Refined sugar alters the pH level in your body (it increases the acidity in your body). When your body pH goes into acidity, the blood struggles to transport oxygen which affects the whole body's metabolism. This results in cells and tissue continuously splitting and growing which creates a perfect environment for bacteria and cancer cells to grow. Refined sugar also impairs healing because it weakens the immune system.

An adequate amount of clean water is vital for good health. A rough estimate of the amount of water that you need is one cup for every 8 kgs that you weigh. Try not to drink water with your meals as the water dilutes the digestive juices, making digestion less efficient. Rather have water an hour before or after your meals.

Surely a slice of 'death by chocolate' cake will not hurt once in a while. There is no verse in the Bible that says 'thou shalt not have any sweets or cakes in thy homes'. But God does speak about living a moderate, self-controlled life and warns us against gluttony. When you eat the right amount of high quality foods with lifegiving nutrients, your body's nutritional needs will be met and you won't feel a 'need' to overeat.

> *"Do not carouse with drunkards or feast with gluttons, for they are on their way to poverty"* (Proverbs 23:20-21).

> *"So, whether you eat or drink, or whatever you do, do it all for the glory of God"* (1 Corinthians 10:31).

When I eat or drink, I always have to be able to say that I am doing it to the benefit of my body and to glorify God.

Consecration

We have read earlier that our bodies are not only the home of our spirit, but also the temple in which the Holy Spirit wants to dwell. As God is holy and set apart, so we must be holy and set apart. We therefore have to live our lives in such a way that we do not defile, contaminate or harm our bodies. God clearly says in His Word that we cannot mix the holy with the unholy.

"And what union can there be between God's temple and idols? For we are the temple of the living God. As God said: I will live in them and walk among them. I will be their God, and they will be my people. Therefore, come out from among the unbelievers, and separate yourselves from them, says the Lord. Don't touch their filthy things and I will welcome you. And I will be your Father, and you will be My sons and daughters, says the Lord Almighty" (2 Corinthians 6:16-18).

There are various ways in which we can defile/contaminate or bring harm to our bodies:

- Self-mutilation (self-harm): e.g. cutting and even some forms of obsessive behaviour/rituals where the body is physically put under immense pressure to perform in order to achieve a certain goal or level of acceptance;

- Sexual sin: Incest, rape, homosexuality, pornography, adultery or fornication. According to God, you become one in flesh with the person you submit to – willing or unwilling. It does not matter whether that person is real or if they are just an image on a screen or in a magazine.

"But you can't say that our bodies were made for sexual immorality. They were made for the Lord and the Lord cares about our bodies. And don't you realize that if a

man joins himself to a prostitute, he becomes one body with her? For the Scriptures say, 'The two are united into one.' Run from sexual sin! No other sin so clearly affects the body as this one does. For sexual immorality is a sin against your own body" (1 Corinthians 6:13-18).

Oral/anal sex, masturbation, etc. is not rooted in love, but in lust (satisfying a physical need at the cost of your own purity and somebody else's freewill or wellbeing). At the core, this forms part of occult practices which makes it unacceptable even in marriage.

> *"Marriage is honourable in every respect; and, in particular, sex within marriage is pure. But God will indeed punish fornicators and adulterers"* (Hebrews 13:4).

When not kept pure for the purpose which God intended it, it brings a number of diseases and harm to the body. Bacterial and viral infections, gum diseases etc. are often consequences of inappropriate sexual practices.

Eating disorders, substance abuse and addictions.

Tattoos: God does not forbid tattoos in the Torah (the Law and the Prophets) because He does not have a good reason for it. It is/was part of pagan ceremonial rituals:
- Honouring the dead;
- Worship to the goddess Neith (ancient 'mother of the gods', also known as the goddess of war and hunting in ancient Egypt (Tutu is 'son of Neith,' 'the Lion', 'Great of Strength' – often depicted as a lion/sphinx);
- Primitive tribes use tattoo marks as means of identification in the next world and a passport to future happiness;
- Mohave Indians instituted tattooing for both sexes because it was believed that a type of judge looks over each one who comes to the land of the dead and if a man does not have marks on his face, he will be sent down to where the 'desert rats' are.

- Sun god worship involves tattooing the hands as a 'divine' token in a mystic attempt to acquire strength (demonic strength – not from the Holy Spirit).

Tattooing had originated in connection with ancient rites of scarification and bloodletting that were associated with religious practices which intended to unite the human soul with supernatural forces and to bring continuity between this life and the next.

This brought not only physical, but also spiritual defilement (demonic influence). Still today, similar rituals are seen in tribal and satanic groups, e.g. Baal worship, shamanism, mysticism, heathenism and cannibalism. The interesting thing is that when those people come to faith in Jesus Christ, they want to get rid of their tattoos because of their understanding of the spiritual significance.

The following summarized comments and descriptions are from pro-tattoo books simply documenting the obvious spiritual and religious link to the tattoo. These are not Christian writers trying to paint a negative portrait of the tattoo:

Tattooing is often a magical rite in the more traditional cultures and the tattooist is respected as a priest or shaman. A shaman is an intermediary between the natural and supernatural worlds, using magic to cure illness, foretell the future, control spiritual forces, etc. *In Fiji, Formosa, New Zealand and in certain of the North American Indian tribes, tattooing was regarded as a religious ceremony and performed by priests or priestesses.*

When the designs are chosen with care, tattoos have a power and magic all on their own. They decorate the body but they also 'enhance' the soul.

Skulls and images of the grim reaper are commonly seen on the skin. These images reflect uncertainty about the future and fear of the unknown. Possibly, at the same time, to wear a death's figure on one's body may be an invocation of whatever undefinable forces of nature and the cosmos that exist, in an attempt to protect the wearer from such a fate. Death and darkness have always been a classic tattoo theme – skulls, snakes, demons, spiders and spider webs are all conventional tattoo imagery. Dark-side tattooing takes our fascination with mortality, death, isolation, fear and evil to new levels. Tattoos act as protective and empowering talismans for the wearer. There are even some body artists who perform ritual tattoos, piercings, brandings and cuttings. Whenever missionaries encountered tattooing, they eradicated it.

It's very interesting that Leviticus 19:28 links the tattoo with 'the dead'. Care to take a wild guess what the number one theme of tattoos is – even in today's modern, civilized, society? Who is the author of death? Who in the Bible is named 'Death'? Satan.

> *"And I looked, and behold a pale horse: and his name that sat on him was Death, and Hell followed with him"* (Revelation 6:8).

Jesus says:
> *"The thief cometh not, but for to steal, and to kill, and to destroy: I have come that they might have life, and that they might have it more abundantly"* (John 10:10).

> In the Word, God clearly warns us not to do what the pagan nations do and to not embrace the ways in which they worship their gods.

> *"...because they are filled [with customs] from the east..."* (Isaiah 2:6)

> *"See to it that no one carries you off as spoil or makes you yourselves captive by his so-called philosophy and intellectualism and vain deceit, following human tradition, just crude notions following the rudimentary and elemental*

*teaching of the universe and disregarding [the teachings of]
Christ the Messiah"* (Colossians 2:8).

*"Don't copy the behaviour and customs of this world, but let
God transform you into a new person by changing the way
you think. Then you will learn to know God's will for you,
which is good and pleasing and perfect"* (Romans 12:2).

Yet we see an increase in people having tattoo upon tattoo, because
it is so 'cool'. In their ignorance, they are giving their bodies to
the enemy and his demons to influence and as a contact point to
operate from.

Remember that Jesus (under the new covenant) has not done
away with the law, but He came to fulfil it so that we do not suffer
the curse of sin, which is death. The Torah was given to us as
a guideline in order to protect us physically and spiritually. Also
remember that there is no condemnation for those who are in
Jesus and in Him there is complete forgiveness of sin. We will be
looking more into that in chapters 5 and 6.

The spirit and soul do not function without the body; therefore,
when physical death occurs, the spirit and soul return to God and
the body turns to dust again.

"For as the body without the spirit is dead..." (James 2:26).

*"If God should set His heart upon him [man] and withdraw
His [life-giving] spirit and His breath [from man] to Himself,
all flesh would perish together, and man would turn again
to dust"* (Job 34:14-15).

"for dust you are and to dust you shall return" (Genesis 3:19).

Your body is your temporary 'home' in which you and the Holy
Spirit dwell – until God gives you a new eternal resurrected body

after physical death on earth.

The Soul

The soul also consists of three parts. They are identified as the mind, the will and the emotions. Let's look at these parts briefly:

1. The Mind

The mind is not the brain. Although the mind is physically in your brain, the mind is separate from the brain and influences the physical brain. Your mind is so incredibly powerful. God has created us with a sound mind. You have a mind that is able to achieve what your dreams are and you can use your mind to be as intelligent as you want to be.

The mind includes:

• *Conscious Mind*
This is the state of awareness, being aware of external factors and being aware of oneself. It is the executive control system of the mind.

• *Subconscious Mind*
The subconscious mind is a composite of everything one sees, hears and any information the mind collects that it cannot otherwise consciously process to make meaningful sense. The conscious mind cannot always absorb disconnected information, as it would be an information overload, so the subconscious mind stores this information where it can be retrieved by the conscious mind when it needs to. The idea of the subconscious as a powerful or potent agency has allowed the term to become prominent in New Age and self-help literature, in which investigating or controlling its supposed knowledge or power is seen as advantageous. Psychologists and psychiatrists take a much more limited view of the capabilities of the unconscious than are represented by New Age depiction of the subconscious. There are a number of methods in use, e.g.

subliminal messages, awakening, trances, autosuggestion and hypnosis. These self-help/New Age methods are not Biblical and can lead to the creation of false memories and demonic influence.

- *Unconscious Mind*

The unconscious mind consists of the processes in the mind that occur automatically and are not available for introspection. They include thought processes, memory, affect and motivation. The unconscious mind includes repressed feelings, automatic skills, subliminal perceptions, thoughts, habits, automatic reactions and hidden phobias and desires. Unconscious processes are understood to be expressed in dreams in a symbolical form, as well as in things we have said; sarcasm or jokes; (Ever said something and afterwards thought 'Where did that come from?'). Thus, the unconscious mind can be seen as the source of dreams and automatic thoughts (those which appear without any apparent cause). It also includes the repository of forgotten memories (which may still be accessible to consciousness at some later time) and implicit knowledge (the things which we have learned so well that we do them without thinking). Sleepwalking and comas may signal the presence of unconscious processes. These processes are not the unconscious mind itself, but rather symptoms. We often see sleepwalking in adults as a result of childhood trauma.

- *Thoughts*

Your mind receives information taken in through your five senses (see, hear, touch, smell and taste). Your five senses are the contact between the external world around you and the internal world of your mind. This information comes in as sound waves and light waves which travel along the nerves in your brain. These light and sound waves are converted into electrical current which now become the thoughts and images in your mind.

The way you think will change the way your brain functions, which has a direct effect on your physical health. If you think in a negative way, you will affect your brain in a negative way. Your incredible, complex brain is subservient to what you do with your mind. So, if you have a thought that says, "I am not going to make it.", well... then you won't make it. Thoughts are powerful and have the creative ability to shape your life. If your mind is dominated by negative thoughts coming from fear, anxiety, unforgiveness, bitterness, anger or self-hatred, your hypothalamus is going to respond by producing either insufficient or excessive quantities of chemicals which then become toxic and harmful for you. This alters the structure of existing memories which, over a period of time through the mind-body connection, leads to the development of disorder and disease.

> *"As a man thinks in his heart, so does he become [so is he]"* (Proverbs 23:7).

- *Memory*

This is the process wherein thoughts (information taken through your five senses) are processed and stored on the branches of the nerves in your brain. The nerve cells (neurons) in your brain look like little trees with branches. A new branch is made for every new piece of information. The more you meditate on a thought, more branches form which make the connections between the branches and the nerves stronger. This strong connection ensures that memory becomes permanent. A strong memory can be a good memory which you can use to improve your life; or it can be a bad (negative) memory – a stronghold in your mind – which can have a negative effect on every part of who and what you are.

> *"For the weapons of our warfare are not carnal, but mighty through God to the pulling down of strongholds; Casting down imaginations, and every high thing that exalteth itself against the knowledge of God, and bringing into captivity every thought to the obedience of Christ"* (2 Corinthians 10:4-5).

The human brain has on average 100 billion nerves and each nerve (tree) can grow up to 200,000 branches. These memory trees are located in the cortex of the brain.

- *Reasoning*

This is the capacity for consciously making sense of things; applying logic; establishing and verifying facts; changing or justifying practices, institutions and beliefs – based on new or existing information (existing memory).

- *Imagination*

This is the ability to form new images and sensations in the mind that are not perceived through senses such as sight, hearing or other senses. Imagination, because of having freedom from external limitations, can often become a source of real pleasure, unnecessary suffering (fear-based expectations which are not real) or an escape from current traumatic situations. Changes to brain chemistry, through hypnosis or other altered states of consciousness, meditation, hallucinogenic drugs and electricity applied directly to specific parts of the brain, causes heightened imagination in people.

The Will

Once the information enters your brain in the form of electric currents (thoughts), it reaches a little sausage shaped structure at the front of the corpus callosum. This is the part in your brain where decision making takes place. This is the physical part in your brain called 'free will'. For example, if you switch on the television and an inappropriate sexual scene comes up, the information comes through your eyes (light waves) and ears (sound waves) that are converted to electrical current in the nerves of your brain. The information is now a thought which reaches your free will. Your free will enables you to make a choice to either allow your brain to meditate on that thought or reject it. If you choose to reject that information, it will literally disappear and will not penetrate your mind. If, however, you choose to meditate on it a little more, it will penetrate the mind to form memory and your brain will respond accordingly, releasing hormones and chemicals. This will result in more lustful thoughts and fantasizing, not only resulting in the very well-known struggle between the flesh and the spirit, but ultimately creating a stronghold of lust and perversion in your mind.

God has given us a will to enable us to freely make choices in life. No manipulation, no control, no intimidation. That is such an act of trust and love. He is asking us to choose life or death, blessing or curse, to love Him or not to love Him and yet the cry of His heart is for us to have an intimate love relationship with Him.

The Emotions

Emotions are complex feelings that result in physical and psychological changes that influence our behaviour.

The part of the brain that is critical in creating the feeling of emotion is the amygdala (an almond shaped mass of cells located deep within the brain). It allows for stress hormones to strengthen neuron (nerve cell) communication. The chemicals cortisone and adrenaline are released in the brain when the amygdala is activated by positive or negative excitement. Throughout your body, you have 'information-emotion molecules'. These molecules in the bloodstream bind to the receptors of the body cells and carry a copy of the memory and the emotion linked to a specific thought/ memory. When a memory is reactivated, the emotion linked to that memory can be physically felt. Have you ever had a memory (of a person who upset you or a fearful experience) and suddenly an emotion has overwhelmed you that you can feel physically? God created us with emotions (in His likeness) and with the ability to express these emotions in a Godly manner. We all have emotional needs and need to be affirmed, accepted and comforted. We need to respect the emotions of others. If you cannot express emotions, you cannot be you.

In summary:

What we think has a direct effect on our emotions, reactions and our physical wellbeing. Every thought (good or bad) stimulates impulses along the nerves in the brain which are responsible for the production of hormones and chemicals secreted throughout your body. Your endocrine system, immune system, nerves, gastro-intestinal system, cardio vascular system, bones and muscles react to these secretions of hormones and chemicals. This process, also known as the mind-body connection, will determine your quality of health and wellbeing.

> *"A happy heart is good medicine and a cheerful mind works healing"* (Proverbs 17:22).

> *"Beloved, I wish above all things that you may prosper and be in health even as your soul prospers"* (3 John v 2).

Now it makes more sense when Paul tells us to constantly renew our minds and to change our thinking. Science calls this process of renewing your mind neuroplasticity or 'retranscribing those memories neuroplastically'. It is the process of detoxifying your brain and changing its neuro-chemical structure by changing your thought life.

> *"Do not be conformed to this world, but be transformed (changed) by the [entire] renewal of your mind [by its new ideals and its new attitude], so that you may prove [for yourselves] what is the good and acceptable and perfect will of God, even the thing which is good and acceptable and perfect [in His sight for you]"* (Romans 12:2).

> *"And be constantly renewed in the spirit of your mind [having a fresh mental and spiritual attitude]"* (Ephesians 4:23).

Through repentance, forgiveness and dealing with emotions

connected to bad (negative) memory, you can change the memory and the structure of the nerve in your brain. The chemicals released by good (positive) thoughts, flows over the negative memory and changes its structure. New memory is built in the place of a negative memory and healing can begin. With the help of the Holy Spirit, you can break those strongholds which have brought disorder and limitation in your body and in your soul.

"For although we do live in the world, we do not wage war in a worldly way; because the weapons we use to wage war are not worldly. On the contrary, they have God's power for demolishing strongholds. We demolish arguments and every arrogance that raises itself up against the knowledge of God; we take every thought captive and make it obey the Messiah" 2 Corinthians 10: 3-5.

The Human Brain affected by Trauma

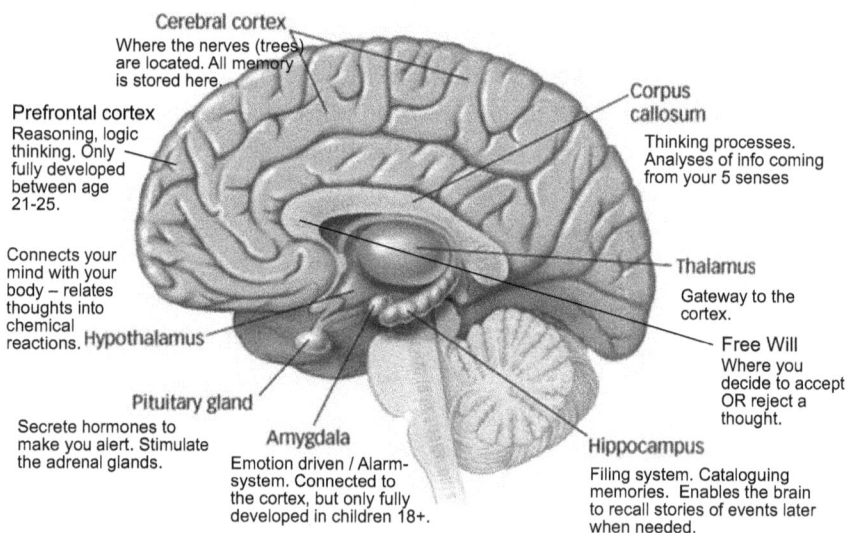

Cerebral cortex
Where the nerves (trees) are located. All memory is stored here.

Prefrontal cortex
Reasoning, logic thinking. Only fully developed between age 21-25.

Connects your mind with your body – relates thoughts into chemical reactions. Hypothalamus

Pituitary gland
Secrete hormones to make you alert. Stimulate the adrenal glands.

Amygdala
Emotion driven / Alarm-system. Connected to the cortex, but only fully developed in children 18+.

Corpus callosum
Thinking processes. Analyses of info coming from your 5 senses

Thalamus
Gateway to the cortex.

Free Will
Where you decide to accept OR reject a thought.

Hippocampus
Filing system. Cataloguing memories. Enables the brain to recall stories of events later when needed.

The HUMAN Spirit

Commonly used metaphors by New Age movements or Eastern religions include the 'voice within', 'the force/power within' and the 'inner light'. The Word of God, however, talks about 'spirit of man' or the 'inner man'.

Our eternal spiritual life comes from God as He gave Adam 'the kiss of life'. As God breathes His life into us, we become living spiritual beings. That is what makes us so unique and different from other living creatures.

> *"And the LORD God formed man of the dust of the ground, and breathed into his nostrils the breath of life; and man became a living soul"* (Genesis 2:7).

> *"...the LORD, which stretcheth forth the heavens, and layeth the foundation of the earth, and formeth the spirit of man within him"* (Zechariah 12:1).

> *"May He grant you out of the rich treasury of His glory to be strengthened and reinforced with mighty power in the inner man by the Holy Spirit [Himself indwelling your innermost being and personality]"* (Ephesians 3:16).

God breathed (literally means a puff of air – like blowing out a candle) His Spirit (Breath of Life) into man and man became a living soul (a living being/person). This puff of air gives us our spiritual 'form'/nature. It is not life sustaining, that is why God says we need a continuous infilling of his Spirit to give us power and to sustain us. God gives us a part of Him in order to live spiritually. Our human spirit is the life source which comes from God at conception.

> *"And be not drunk with wine, wherein is excess; but be filled (G4137 – having one's appetite excessively satisfied; perfect supply) with the Spirit"* (Ephesians 5:18).

> *"But you shall receive power (ability, efficiency and might) when the Holy Spirit has come upon you, and you shall be My witnesses in Jerusalem and all Judea and Samaria*

and to the ends (the very bounds) of the earth" (Acts 1:8).

The word power is taken from the Greek word 'Dunamis' where we get the word Dynamo/Dynamos (plural) from. According to the dictionary, 'Dynamo' is either a generator or a forceful energetic individual. In other words, to have power/spiritual energy that continually keeps you going (sustains you daily), you have to be connected to the Source that supplies you with that power – not yoga or crystals, but the only True God who has power and authority over ALL created things.

Being continuously filled with the Holy Spirit will not only give us power or energy to run the race of life, but it will also satisfy and sustain us – we do not need the things that this world has to offer which only act as a very cheap substitute and a perversion.

God has created our identity/personhood (who we really are) as part of our human spirit. In life, we mostly identify people through the sound of their voice or what they look like physically. If you know somebody intimately, you would more easily describe them less physically and more personally because you get to know them for who they are – their personality traits, gifting etc.

Humans have two sets of memory/thinking ability, as well as free will and emotions. One set is resident in the spirit and the other in the soul. The spirit has an existence that transcends the body, although it is deeply interrelated with the body. When you go into theatre for surgery, the body is given general anaesthesia. This also precludes the soul from expressing itself. The soul cannot comment on the cold room, the doctor's discussions on Saturday's sports match or wishing the nurse had less makeup on. The soul is not even able to record most of the events in the theatre in order to recall them later and comment on them. In contrast, the spirit is very much aware of what is happening all the time. Often recorded, near death or out of body experiences reveal that the spirit leaves the body and the person looks down on activities around him/her.

Later, the spirit reports on the experience in detail.

The spirit can also be defined in three parts known as Communion, your Conscience and your Intuition.

a. Communion

This is the ability to relate to God on a spiritual level. He is a Spiritual Being and so are we, and we communicate with Him through our spirit. Our worship, how we respond to love, what we believe about ourselves and God and who we believe we are, are determined by our communion with God. It is the Holy Spirit who gives us strength, wisdom, knowledge and understanding in order for us to live out our created purpose.

> *"But there is (a vital force) a spirit (of intelligence) in man, and the Breath of the Almighty gives men understanding"* (Job 32:8).

> *"May He grant you out of the rich treasury of His glory to be strengthened and reinforced with mighty power in the inner man by the [Holy] Spirit [Himself indwelling your innermost being and personality]"* (Ephesians 3:16).

> *"The Spirit Himself testifies together with our own spirit [assuring us] that we are children of God"* (Romans 8:16).

> *"Your righteous testimonies are everlasting and Your decrees are binding to eternity; give me understanding and I shall live (to be whole, to revive)"* (Psalm 119:144).

b. Conscience

As we have communion with God, we become more and more aware of what is right and what is wrong. This awareness in our spirit, which comes from the Holy Spirit, governs our thoughts (soul) and actions.

> *"...I will imprint My laws (of Moses and the Gospel) upon their innermost thoughts and understanding, and engrave them upon their hearts; and I will be their God, and they shall be My people."* (Hebrews 8:10).

> *"... because the mind of the flesh [with its carnal thoughts and purposes] is hostile to God, for it does not submit itself to God's Law (of Moses and the Gospel); But you are not living the life of the flesh, you are living the life of the Spirit, if the [Holy] Spirit of God dwells within you [directs and controls you]"* (Romans 8:7,9).

> *"I am not lying; my conscience [enlightened and prompted] by the Holy Spirit bearing witness with me"* (Romans 9:1).

c. Intuition

This is an instinctive belief or knowledge, a hunch, a 'gut feeling'. It is when you experience a deep knowing (in your spirit), not obtained by reasoning or perception (mind or emotion). You just know, because you know.

Up to now, you can see how amazingly complex yet functional we are as created beings, each part working in harmony with one another in order for us to live life in its fullness, but also to help us cope in stressful or harmful situations.

In Scripture, we can see a clear description of body, soul and spirit; how they relate to one another and how they have an effect on one another.

Here are some examples:

In Hebrew:

> *"For the enemy hath persecuted my* soul; *he hath smitten*

my life down to the ground; he hath made me to dwell in darkness, as those that have been long dead. Therefore is my spirit *overwhelmed within me; my* heart *within me is desolate"* (Psalm 143:3-4).

"With my soul *have I desired Thee in the night; yea, with my* spirit *within me will I seek Thee early"* (Isaiah 26:9).

Soul = H5315 – Nephesh (mind)
Spirit = H7307 – Ruach (breath of life/spirit of a rational being)
Heart = H3820 – Lêb (emotions/feelings)

In Greek:

"And the very God of peace sanctify you wholly; and I pray God your whole spirit *and* soul *and* body *be preserved blameless unto the coming of our Lord Jesus Christ"* (1 Thessalonians 5:23).

"For the Word of God is quick, and powerful, and sharper than any two edged sword, piercing even to the dividing asunder of soul *and* spirit, *and of the* joints and marrow, *and is a discerner of the thoughts and intents of the* heart*"* (Hebrews 4:12).

Soul = G5590 – Psuchē (mind).
Spirit = G4151 – Pneuma (breath of life/rational immortal soul).
Joints and Marrow = The body.
Heart = G2588 – Kardia (feelings and thoughts).

All human beings experience life in different ways, all dependant on our beliefs, perceptions and, of course, our relationship with the Only True God. Now, you may ask the question: How does the spiritual which we experience become physical?

Our spirit hears three different voices (in the spirit). The Voice of God (Holy Spirit), the voice of the enemy (satan and his kingdom because they are also spirits) and our own spirit. Our theta brain waves discern (hear/comprehend) voices or impressions on a spiritual level. These theta brain waves relate this voice (message) which we hear to our brain which becomes a thought. The thought then also travels to our free will from where we can choose to either accept it or to reject it.

The same thing happens when people in certain cultures do their trance dances on drum beats. At four and a half drum beats per second, the theta waves are activated and it creates a pathway for the person to connect with the spiritual realm. This way, they can connect with the 'ancestors' (demonic spirits) and gain spiritual 'knowledge'. Hallucinogenic drugs have the same effect on the theta brain waves and causes trans-like states where people are exposed to the spiritual realm.

Young children have very active theta brain waves and are very sensitive to the spirit realm. Their human spirit is very alert and still uncluttered. Often children will say that they see 'things' at night or have imaginary friends. These can very well be visitations from the demonic who try to connect with them in a way that is less frightening.

> *"And do not marvel; for satan himself is transformed into an angel of light"* (2 Corinthians 11:14).

The spirit was designed to lead and it needs to know that. It was designed by God to bring healing and nurture to the soul. This can only happen when the spirit is legitimized and comes to a place of dominion.

> *"The spirit of man [the factor in human personality which proceeds immediately from God] is the lamp of the Lord, searching all his innermost parts"* (Proverbs 20:27).

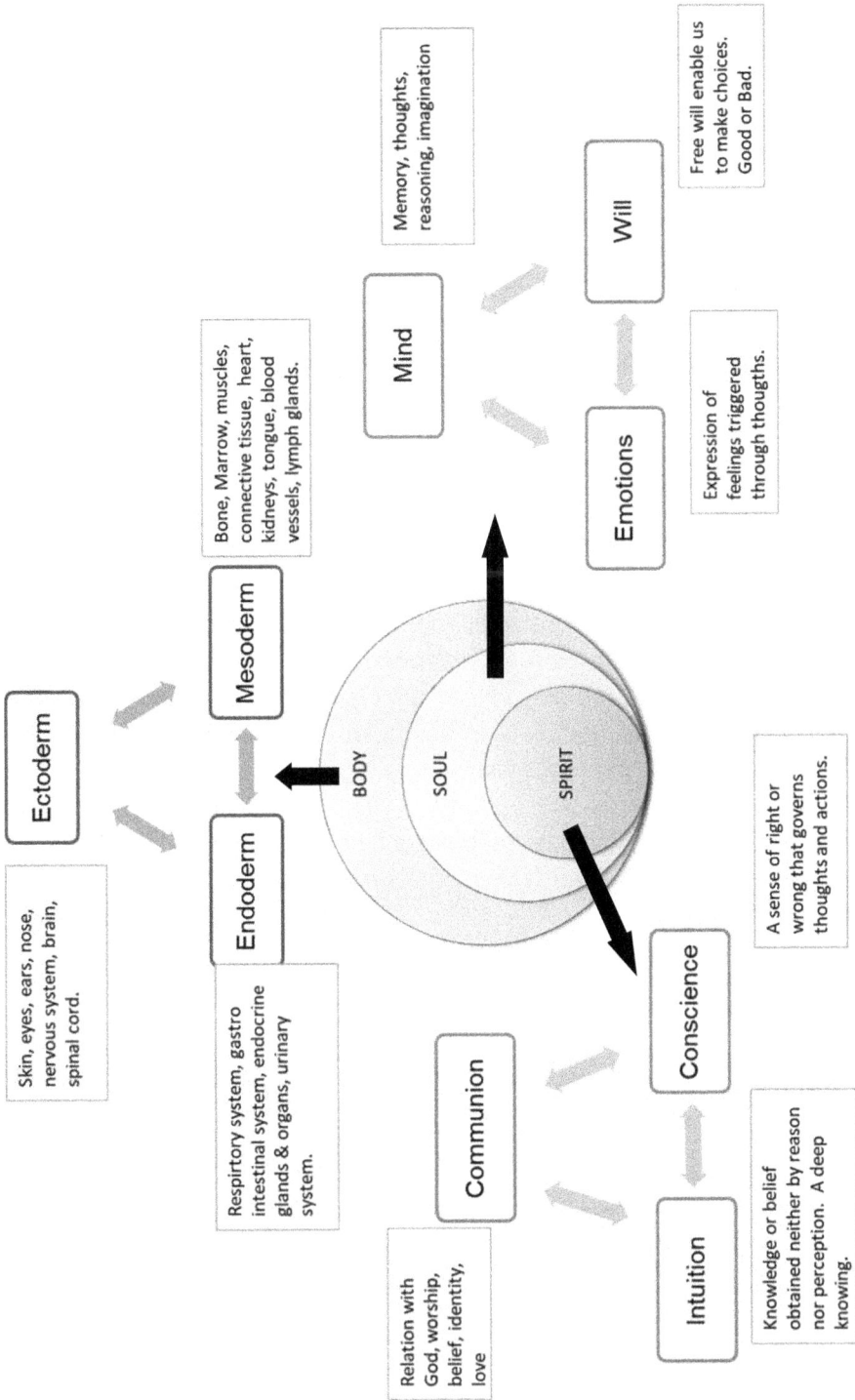

Memory, thoughts, reasoning, imagination

Free will enable us to make choices. Good or Bad.

Will

Mind

Bone, Marrow, muscles, connective tissue, heart, kidneys, tongue, blood vessels, lymph glands.

Emotions

Expression of feelings triggered through thoughts.

Mesoderm

BODY

SOUL

SPIRIT

Ectoderm

Endoderm

A sense of right or wrong that governs thoughts and actions.

Skin, eyes, ears, nose, nervous system, brain, spinal cord.

Respirtory system, gastro intestinal system, endocrine glands & organs, urinary system.

Conscience

Communion

Intuition

Knowledge or belief obtained neither by reason nor perception. A deep knowing.

Relation with God, worship, belief, identity, love

Chapter 3

Brokenness

If we want to define brokenness, we first need to see what it means to be whole because, if you are not in a place of wholeness, you are experiencing brokenness in some area of your life.

According to the Collins dictionary, the word 'whole' means: Containing all the component parts necessary for a total; Complete; Uninjured or undamaged; Healthy; Having no fractional part; Undivided; A thing complete in itself; An assemblage of parts (a number of things put together) viewed together as a unit.

Wellness (looking after your physical health and fitness) is not wholeness, but wholeness does include wellness.

> "Physical training is good, but training for godliness is much better promising benefits in this life and in the life to come" (1 Timothy 4:8).

According to the Word of God, 'whole' or 'wholeness' is seen as the following:
> "And may the God of peace Himself sanctify you through and through [separate you from profane things, make you pure and wholly consecrated to God]; and may your spirit and soul and body be preserved sound and complete [and found] blameless at the coming of our Lord Jesus Christ [the Messiah]" (1 Thessalonians 5:23).

G3650/G3651= holos – wholly: all, altogether, complete to the end, absolutely perfect.

In conclusion, we can say that wholeness means that every part of our being (body, soul and spirit), every part of what makes me, is functioning in unity (all together, not divided) without injury, without damage, without any fractional parts and completely sound.

God urges us to keep every part of who/what He created pure, set apart and preserved (safe from harm or danger, protected from decay, maintained) until Jesus returns for His Bride.

This brings us to the rude awakening that practically no Christian is completely whole. We surely are all works in progress as the Scripture above clearly states. What are the things that bring injury, damage or cause us to have fractional parts? In short – Life after the fall!

Let us take a look at how life experiences can lead to brokenness in every part of our being. We were all created for love by a God who is Love. When we experience His perfect love (demonstrated through our parents) from the day of conception, our human spirit knows perfect love and experiences a deep sense of belonging. We feel secure, safe and wanted. In the womb, the embryo experiences a sense of welcoming, nurturing and love and develops into a whole person. We grow physically and emotionally according to the message that our spirit conveys to our soul. Our spirit expresses itself through the soul and the body reacts according to what it has received from the soul.

From the time of conception, the spirit forms core beliefs according to what it is exposed to. Up to the age of about eight years old, a child forms core beliefs, mindsets and thinking patterns about who they are, where they belong, what people think of them, if they are safe and, most of all, what they think about God. These processes first occur in the human spirit and then in the soul area and determine our perception of identity, calling and destiny.

A baby cannot offer much and cannot do anything for you to receive something in return. Yet in knowing that, a baby is so utterly dependant on the parents and is like a little sponge, sucking up every bit of attention, affection and love it is exposed to. Unfortunately, the flip-side of the coin is also true – we suck up everything negative which we are exposed to.

An anxious expectant mother does not realize that her unborn baby, first and foremost, needs to find and know his/her connection with Mom above his/her need for food. There is a deep longing within the spirit of an embryo to know and to be known. It has to know both who and whose it is. This little human spirit must know that there is a safe and intimate connection for him/her in this vast expansive world. Ideally, this connection should first happen in our homes and then in other ways as we grow up into adulthood.

From conception, every human being needs nurture. Nurture literally means to give tender care and protection to a child, helping him/her to grow and develop, thrive and be successful. This is vital if this little one is going to flourish; for without this link, it is very easy to lose his/her way. You can't allow just anyone to define you. You should not ask just anybody/anything who you are or whom you belong to. If parents do not nurture their children, they raise sons and daughters who are self-focused, self-contained, disconnected survivors. They become individuals who have the capacity to function but lack the power to flourish. As parents, we should pursue a heart connection with our children in order to form an intimate bond that secures them in love. As we gaze into the 'mirror' of God and behold the image which He is reflecting back at us, we in return are reflecting that image of love, acceptance and affirmation back at our children. They peer into our faces, hoping to catch reflections of themselves. What will they see reflected in your eyes? In your words? In your embrace?

We are not nurturing when we limit our children to what we see in, or believe about them. We are wrong if we set them up to expect too little or something different of them than what God speaks over them. Our children will inherit our fears of God's promises. Our disappointments, fears and insecurities are our own stories, not theirs. Never limit your children by comparing them to yourself.

They want us to look into their young, vulnerable lives and behold the promises of God and be proud of them. God did not entrust them to us for us to live through. They were given life through us so they would go beyond our boundaries on every level.

In previous generations, it was very common for moms to stay at home. Things have changed so much these days. Mom and Dad both work and the children are placed in day care or after-school care. They are entertained with internet, movies, television and games. Most of these entertainments are filled with violence, rage, revenge and far-fetched unreality with no nurture whatsoever. Parents travel on separate paths and do not create quality family time.

God has created us for relationship – our spirits crave intimacy and closeness. All around us today we see people with 'orphaned', 'starved' human spirits. They are calling out for love, safety and affection – running from one thing to another, but far too often these voices go unanswered. These people are in our homes, school systems, marketplace, and churches. They range from young sportsmen to college students, doctors, attorneys and even the pastor's wife, who are surrounded with many people, but deep inside they are alone. Are we far too busy or consumed with our own lives and issues to make the time to assure that the tender lives surrounding us thrive?

Most parents, educational systems and even churches are set up to merely meet the physical needs of people and do not focus on nurturing the human spirit, maybe because we do not have the resources; maybe because the focus is more on the emotions (making people feel good) than on the spiritual wellbeing of the person. Every person's life will enlarge when nurture is added for it is then that these organizations will cease to function – they will begin to flourish, because the people flourish. We are called to more than need-meeting, we are called to build lives and relationships. Unfortunately, we lose our vision (remember the mirror of God) and our true sense of worth and identity.

Too many of us, in the church, were intimately wounded, disappointed and betrayed by those who were entrusted to nurture and protect us. We sought nurture and instead we were oppressed, neglected, deprived, controlled, abused and fed lies instead of God's truth. This is what happens when humans have lost their heavenly connection and perspective. If you experienced a violation of safety or trust where you should have had nurture, it is still imperative that these intimate connections happen.

God has put together our personhood with specifically matching gifting and calling in order for us to fulfil our destiny. Identity plus calling equals destiny (Identity + calling = destiny). Our destiny and our identity give us value, self-worth and a sense of belonging. If we do not know who we are and why God has created us in a specific way, we cannot fulfil our true destiny. Knowing yourself first is important before you recognise your calling and destiny.

We were created to be a delight to God – to have relationship with Him, to dwell with Him as sons and daughters. This is our primary calling. We were never created to work for Him. If I were to ask you, "Who are you?" what would you answer? "I am a doctor"; "I am a pastor"; "I am a mother"; "I am a prophet". You see, God made *you,* before He made you a doctor or a pastor or a mother or a prophet. The function, job or expectations you fulfil in life are not who you are. If you take all your responsibilities and expectations (your own and what other people put on you) out of the way, who are you then? It is quite easy to answer from a place where you know in your head that you are a son/daughter of Father God, because you have read it in the Bible and you have heard it so often, but do you know it deep down in your spirit? If you are unable to answer that question, I encourage you to ask God to show you if there is damage or brokenness in your spirit. God knows your spirit.

> *"Before I formed you in the womb I* knew *and approved of you [as My chosen instrument] and before you were born I separated and set you apart, consecrating you; and I appointed you as a prophet to the nations"* (Jeremiah 1:5).

H3045 = yâda' – to *know* (properly to ascertain by *seeing*); *observation, care, recognition.* God couldn't have known Jeremiah in this way before he was physically formed in the womb, but God knew his spirit – who Jeremiah really was as a son. God also put His calling and destiny in place because of who Jeremiah was. This was long before Jeremiah could do or prove anything to anybody. God did not only choose Jeremiah, He chose every single one of us because He created us.

Maybe you have fallen into the same pit I did and compared yourself to everybody around you all your life. 'I am not as beautiful, or as smart, or as important as the person next to me'; 'I cannot articulate my words so well, so I'd rather keep quiet'; 'I am not as prophetic as that person'; 'I am a victim'. These thought patterns can be so real and so toxic. They were formed because of wounding and I have partnered with them and believed them. It determined the course of my life and I went round and round the same mountain for many years in my life.

Your spirit reflects who you really are and if there is brokenness, that is what will be expressed through your soul and your body. That part, deep inside of you, knows who you are.

> *"As a face is reflected in water, so the heart reflects the real person"* (Proverbs 27:19).

Heart = Lêb; inner man, core or centre of something.

> *"For who knows a person's thoughts except their own spirit*

within them? In the same way no one knows the thoughts of God except the Spirit of God" (1 Corinthians 2:11).

"The spirit of man [that factor in human personality which proceeds immediately from God] is the lamp of the Lord, searching all his innermost parts" (Proverbs 20:27).

We were created in the likeness of God. In the same manner in which His Spirit knows all things, so does our human spirit know all things from the time of conception. It is so important to know your spirit and what the condition is of your spirit. Do you allow your spirit to speak or do your thoughts and emotions speak all the time? Which part of you is in control of your life? The Godly order in our lives should be for our spirit to connect with His Spirit and, as a result of revelation and intimacy with Him, we lead our life by the Spirit.

"...to be strengthened with might by his Spirit in the inner man;" (Ephesians 3:16).

"You are controlled by the Spirit if you have the Spirit of God living in you" (Romans 8:9).

"For if you live by its (sinful nature) dictates, you will die. But if through the power of the Spirit you put to death the deeds of your sinful nature, you will live. For all who are led by the Spirit of God are children of God" (Romans 8:13-14).

"I the Lord search the mind, I try the heart, even to give to every man according to his ways, according to the fruit of his doings" (Jeremiah 17:10).

As the Holy Spirit strengthens and feeds your spirit, your spirit will become strong and healthy and this will enable you to lead a life of fruitfulness and wholeness. When there is damage or fractional parts in the human spirit, it is very difficult for the spirit to take control because it is broken/damaged.

What causes brokenness?

Lack of nurture, lack of protection, domination, control, fear, anxiety, neglect, cruelty, abuse, false expectations, shame and guilt are all experiences which damage the spirit and have an influence on the development of a person.

Sometimes people decide who you should be because that is how they see you or that is the trait in the family line, e.g. 'You are going to be....' or 'You must be a .... because that is what we do in this family/culture'. What expectations did people put on you when you were a child? What words did they speak over who you are? As a result, how did these things influence who you are today and what you believe about yourself?

Growing up, you are moulded by the people around you and the experiences you live through from the very beginning. Did you feel nurtured, accepted and loved unconditionally for who you are? Did you feel valued? Did you feel that you were heard (could give your opinion)? Have you ever felt ridiculed? Have you ever felt that you have always been a burden or a disappointment to your family or people close to you? Have you ever felt that you are the wrong sex, that you rather should have been a girl/boy – maybe God made a mistake when He formed your body? Did you ever feel, deep down, that you are not safe?

Those in authority over a person (parents, carers, educators, pastors and spiritual leaders) may abuse their authority by being misunderstanding, overpowering or fear-instilling instead of encouraging unconditional love and acceptance. Often children are not allowed to express emotions and that hinders the child from developing his/her personhood because they cannot be real about who they are and what they feel. The atmosphere in which a person grows affects their ability to grow as God intended. God's love says 'I love you deeply no matter what you do or what you look like.'

Your whole life, you are striving to try and live up to the standards and expectations of others and you never become who you are created to be. You strive for significance, to be a 'somebody'. No one wants to be a 'nobody'. Nothing you do seems good enough for you or for them. It causes so much inner conflict and stress that you become an anxious, unsatisfied, unhappy person. You never follow your dreams or your heart's desires. It crushes your spirit because you were never made for that and, somewhere along the way, you leave behind something of who you really are. You live in an unreality of who you really are – that is deception beautifully packaged.

Adults who are struggling today were neglected, confused, abused, controlled children a few years ago. Many women who are engaged in prostitution were raped or molested as children. A hostile, anger-filled home environment where pornographic material is 'normal' is a breeding place for sexual abusers, perverts and drug addicts. Many homosexuals have been sexually defiled and rejected at a very young age.

The enemy selects his victims when they are children – young, innocent and vulnerable. The enemy is also aware of the importance of spiritual protection in the home and early teaching. At an early age, children are emotionally very sensitive and mentally very impressionable. That is why God clearly instructs us: *"Train up a child in the way he should go, and when he is old he will not depart from it"* (Proverbs 22:6).

The truth of the Word of God must be written on their hearts before the circumstances and pressures from the world form a callus on their hearts.

For any seed to germinate and develop into a strong tree, it needs the perfect environment. In the same way, every person (from conception) needs the perfect environment to grow and develop in who God created them to be. Nobody grows up in a perfect environment because people are not perfect and makes mistakes. As a parent, you might not realize the vital role you play in a child's life, helping them to discover and develop their God-given identity.

Generational defilement and individual sin can represent an immense pile of toxic waste but, in reality, at the core of every believer is the light of God. For a highly troubled soul, knowing that the fingerprint of God is still visible on their spirit is hugely validating, comforting and giving that person hope.

In the family of God, there is a perfect Father who delights in who you are. God created each person with potential, gifting and a calling to fulfil the destiny one has been created for. Your spirit (personhood) needs development. For so long you have looked in faulty mirrors and had a distorted view of yourself.

Are you ready for change? Are you ready to give the Father that part you are clinging to that is not part of who you are? Allow God to teach you who you really are. That is why Jesus died and was raised to life again!

> *"They that be whole need not a physician, but they that are sick (worthless, depraved, injurious, evil, harm)"* (Matthew 9:12).

> *"...He has sent me to bind up and heal the broken-hearted..."* (Isaiah 61:1).

Jesus Christ was sent by the Father to bring healing and wholeness to every part of who we are.

How do the body and soul relate or respond to brokenness in the human spirit?

I want to show you from the Bible how these parts influence and reflect each other when we are exposed to the words and actions of others (coming out of pride, resentment, and bitterness), traumatic events, or abuse. I also want to show you how modern medical science aligns with the Word of God in many ways.

> *"A gentle tongue [with its healing power] is a tree of life, but wilful contrariness in it breaks down the spirit"* (Proverbs 15:4).

shâbar = break, fracture, ruin

> *"Insults and reproach* (disgrace, shame) *have broken* (crushed, quenched) *my heart* (emotions); *I am full of heaviness and I am distressingly sick* (body)*"* (Psalm 69:20).

> *"A sound* (healthy, wholesome) *heart* (emotions) *is the life of the flesh (body): but envy (jealousy) the rottenness* (decay) *of the bones"* (Proverbs 14:30).

> *"I am exhausted from crying for help; humiliation is written all over my face. Their insults have broken my heart, and I am in despair. If only one person would show some pity; if only one would turn and comfort me. I am suffering and in pain."* (Psalm 69).

> *"My spirit is broken; my days are spent; the grave is ready for me. Surely there are mockers and mockery around me; and my eye dwells on their obstinacy, insults and resistance"* (Job 17:1-2).

Our words can bring life, but the humiliating, harsh, unloving spoken words of people around us can ruin/fracture our spirit (true identity/personhood). We can often see in 'body language' (body movement and facial expressions) and hear in their vocabulary when people are sad, angry, bitter, resentful or jealous. The Word says that it brings decay to the bones – it brings despair, suffering and pain. During our pain, we often seek love, acceptance and comfort, but we end up looking in the wrong places. We fill our lives with strife and perfectionism, compromising who we really are for anything that will fill the empty hole in our spirits.

"A happy heart [emotions] *is good medicine and a cheerful mind* [thoughts] *works healing, but a broken [smitten, wounded] spirit dries up the bones* [body]" (Proverbs 17:22).

If you are a happy person who knows who you are and who brings your thoughts under the authority of Christ, you will prosper in your health. On the other hand, if your spirit is broken, it has a direct effect on the functioning of your body. What is in your bones? Your bone marrow. What is made in your bone marrow? Your blood – white and red blood cells. In other words – your immune system. If your spirit is broken or overwhelmed due to abuse, trauma or rejection or if your mind is not at peace and you are experiencing stress, anxiety, fear, unforgiveness, resentment, anger, shame, guilt etc., it will eventually break down the body's immune system, causing disease.

> *"The spirit of a man will sustain his infirmity* (physical disease, pain); *but a wounded spirit who can bear?"* (Proverbs 18:14).

I have experienced how people with cancer and identity disorders deal with spiritual, emotional, physical and generational issues and are victorious because they feed their spirit with the truth of God's Word. There is hope and life in the Healer. It is in the time of suffering that they choose to come closer to God. Despite pain or discomfort, they worship God and they are happy people.

> *"Therefore I will not restrain my mouth; I will speak in the anguish of my spirit, I will complain in the bitterness of my soul [O Lord]"* (Job 7:11).

In this text, we can hear how desperate Job is and he finds help, comfort and acceptance in only one place – the presence of the LORD.

According to recent scientific research, it has been evident that in 70% of psychiatric diseases, there is no brain dysfunction or brain damage. In specifically studying the brain, it has been discovered that 87% of all diseases (psychological and physical) are a result of what goes on in our thought life (soul). The mind-body connection, of which psychology speaks, does exist.

This scientific revelation lines up with the Word of God:

> "For as he thinks in his heart (thoughts and emotions), so is he" (Proverbs 23:7).

> "Beloved, I pray that you may prosper in every way and [that your body] may keep well, even as [I know] your soul keeps well and prospers" (3 John 1:2).

As previously stated – if your thought life is filled with fear, anxiety, stress, hate, unforgiveness, bitterness, anger, guilt, shame, drivenness etc. and you meditate on them, the branches (trees) in your brain will become toxic. Your brain reacts to these toxic thoughts and release chemicals and hormones in abnormal quantities which, when prolonged, can be very damaging to the body.

Let us look at fear, guilt and shame:

> "and Adam and his wife hid themselves from the presence of the Lord God... But the Lord God called to Adam and said to him, Where are you? He said, I heard the sound of You [walking] in the garden, and I was afraid because I was naked; and I hid myself" (Genesis 3:8-10).

The unity they had experienced with Father God, with each other and within themselves was disrupted. Fear entered their hearts and brought separation between them and Father God. Guilt separated them from the truth of God (their identity in Him) and shame brought separation in their own hearts/minds. These were the very first consequences of disobedience in the Garden of Eden and it still has such an enormous effect on us today. I do not think there are many, if any, people who can say that they have never before been influenced or tormented by fear, guilt or shame.

Fear

Fear can be a result of trauma, loss and lack of nurture and love. Anything that takes away our freedom, humiliates or intimidates us, produces fear. Fear is the root of anxiety or worry and disrupts the way we function. It is the mind's and body's response to any pressure that disrupts a peaceful state in your spirit (the core of who you are). The result is that you then try to find objects/people to believe or trust in (Adam's fig leaves).

There are different types of fear:
- Superficial fear: fear of meeting deadlines, fear of not having enough money, fear of safety.

- Deep fear: fear of man, fear of trust, fear of abandonment, fear of being alone, fear of being vulnerable, fear of being hurt etc. What opens the door to this type of fear? A result of a lack of nurture and protection, victimization, abuse or a breach in relationships causing insecurity, a lack of peace and a broken heart.

  "Men's hearts failing them for fear" (Luke 21:26).

  "There is no fear in love [dread does not exist], but full-grown (complete, perfect) love turns fear out of doors and expels every trace of terror! For fear brings with it the thought of punishment and [so] he who is afraid has not reached the full maturity of love [is not yet grown into love's complete perfection]" (1 John 4:18).

This is such a powerful scripture! What it basically says is that if you have been loved conditionally (based on performance, false expectations, not loved for who you are as a person), or physically, sexually or emotionally abused, fear is knocking at your door...for sure! With that fear come terror and thoughts of punishment.

Have you ever experienced (or know of somebody who has) vivid nightmares or panic attacks? That is torment. If you are living in fear, you have not yet experienced true unconditional, pure, perfect love! There is a huge need to reach the full maturity of perfect love. That is only possible if you allow the Father, who is love, to teach you what love really is – not just knowing in your head – I am talking about a personal experience.

The enemy is not going to come at you unmasked! No, he will come (in the spirit) and speak lies (through your theta brain waves) bringing feelings/impressions of insecurity, drivenness, perfectionism, low self-esteem, fear of man, fear of failure, fear of death, fear of punishment, fear of getting hurt, and the list goes on....

When your body is in a constant fight or flight state because of constant fear, anxiety and stress; excessive cortisol (a steroid hormone released from the adrenal glands in response to stress) is released. The oversecretion of cortisol has a direct physiological effect on the following functions:

- Carbohydrate and lipid metabolism, protein metabolism, inflammatory effects, lipid function, muscle function, bone function, vascular system, myocardial and the central nervous system function.
- Cortisol directly influences immune responses to antibodies. The oversecretion of cortisol destroys the immune system resulting in disease.

"For God did not give us a spirit of timidity (cowardice, of craven and cringing and fawning fear), but He has given us a spirit of power and of love and of calm and well-balanced mind and discipline and self-control" (2 Timothy 1:7).

Another translation of this Scripture reads: *"For God has not given us a spirit of fear, but of power and of love and of a sound mind."*

Can you see that fear has a direct effect on our mind? Where there is fear, there is no balance (soundness), no discipline and no self-control and, most of all, no maturity in pure love. As we grow in our knowledge and relationship with God, our faith grows. Faith is equal and opposite to fear.

"Faith is the substance of things hoped for, the evidence of things not seen" (Hebrews 11:1).

Fear is the substance of things NOT hoped for, the evidence not yet seen.

God has given every person a measure of faith (Romans 12:3) and as we mature spiritually, our faith increases.

Because of trauma, loss, breach in relationships or brokenness, we don't always live in faith. Fear is not only an emotion, but also a demonic force that triggers more than over a thousand known harmful physical and chemical responses in your body.

Faith and a growing intimate relationship (perfect love) with God defeats fear. The only Godly, 'safe' fear mentioned in the Word is the fear of the LORD.

"The fear of the LORD is the beginning of wisdom" (Psalm 111:10).

"And unto man he said, Behold, the fear of the Lord, that is wisdom; and to depart from evil is understanding" (Job 28:28).

"The fear of the LORD prolongeth days: but the years of the wicked shall be shortened" (Proverbs 10:27).

"In the fear of the LORD is strong confidence: and his children shall have a place of refuge" (Proverbs 14:26).

If you feel safe, loved and nurtured, you are naturally happy and full of joy, then your body creates endorphins. Endorphins are natural chemicals in the body that fight pain. Endorphins are released when a person gets hurt, but also during exercise, laughter or sex.

In addition to blocking pain, endorphins can make people happy in much higher quantities than medicine can give.

"Restore to me the joy of Your salvation and uphold me with a willing spirit" (Psalm 51:12).

Here are some diseases which can form in the body as a consequence of fear, anxiety and high levels of stress:
- High blood pressure; angina; heart valve disease; heart failure; compromised immune systems causing viruses, bacteria and cancer cells to enter the body cells and cause disease; fatigue; exhaustion; insomnia; phobias; panic attacks; poor memory; indigestion; constipation; diarrhoea; stomach ulcers; reflux; irritable bowel syndrome; ulcerative colitis; fertility problems and irregular menstrual periods; allergies; muscular tension causing headaches, backaches and muscle contractions.

Stress reduces the growth hormone in children. High levels of stress hormones delay healing in the body, causes inflammation and influence the process of bone formation.

Guilt

Guilt and shame are often confusing and people rarely distinguish between the two. Guilt is a belief/feeling as a result of something 'bad' you have done or something you feel you should have done. It is focused on behaviour rather than just emotion. Guilt makes you react according to what you have done and according to your values. You often react in a negative way towards people through thoughts and feelings of hostility, bitterness, accusation, unkindness and rebellion, thus hindering them from giving the very thing that you need – love. If you feel guilty because of something you think you should have done, but did not do (usually because of false expectations), you always try to make up for it in some way, which is usually not a Godly way – you overcompensate. It causes separation in our relationship with God and with other people.

"Exercise foresight and be on the watch to look [after one another], to see that no one falls back from and fails to secure God's grace [His unmerited favour and spiritual blessing], in order that no root of resentment [rancour, bitterness or hatred] shoots forth and causes trouble and bitter torment, and the many become contaminated and defiled by it" (Hebrews 12:15).

"Therefore, [there is] now no condemnation (no adjudging guilty of wrong) for those who are in Christ Jesus, who live [and] walk not after the dictates of the flesh, but after the dictates of the Spirit" (Romans 8:1). Also see John 3:18.

"If we [freely] admit that we have sinned and confess our sins, He is faithful and just (true to His own nature and promises) and will forgive our sins [dismiss our lawlessness] and continuously cleanse us from all unrighteousness [everything not in conformity to His will in purpose, thought, and action] (1 John 1:9).

When we come to Christ and ask for forgiveness of sins (our own), forgive those who have wronged us and ask the Father to cleanse us from these sins, we have taken away the legal right of the enemy to come and torment us with guilt. If the magnificent God of all creation has forgiven you, who are you then to hold yourself guilty over something that has been cleansed by the Blood of His Son, Jesus?

As you harbour and meditate on the guilt (which does not belong to you in the first place), you are actually attacking yourself spiritually and emotionally. Do you still remember mind-body connection? These negative thoughts become permanent memories and your brain and body react to these negative messages. When you are attacking yourself through thoughts of guilt, bitterness, self-accusation and self-condemnation, the biogenetic character of the cells in your immune system changes and the immune system begins to attack your own body tissue and joints. In other words, the immune system, which was designed by God to fight off disease, will now fight against you and cause disease. This is the trigger of many autoimmune diseases. When we live a life of true repentance, we walk in His righteousness and there is then no place for guilt or condemnation.

Shame

This almost feels the same as guilt but it is more a sense of 'I feel bad' or 'I am bad' or 'I am not good enough'. It is essentially created from an ongoing experience of rejection, humiliation, neglect and abuse (trauma). If not recognized and dealt with, it becomes part of who you are – your identity. You operate life out of this belief and it can either make you feel disconnected from other people and create a sense of loneliness (withdrawal), or always trying to shame other people so that you can feel better about yourself.

To keep shame intact or to defend it consumes excessive amounts of energy. It results in a lack of self-worth (self-esteem); always comparing yourself with others and in time it leads to addictions, unfaithfulness, envy, harshness and pride. A low self-esteem can lead you into a range of addictions in order to try and find comfort, relief and satisfaction. Whether it is caffeine, prescription drugs, food or sex, the one thing will lead to the next and just create more fear, more guilt and more shame. You do something you know you should not be doing to feel better, then you feel guilty because of what you have done and then the shame ('I am bad') follows – a repetitive cycle that keeps you in bondage. We learn various coping mechanisms to try and fight the shame we feel.

When you are in this toxic state of shame, excessive amounts of cortisol (stress hormone) is continuously secreted, damaging your internal organs e.g. lungs, liver and intestines.

Shame survives on secrecy, judgement and darkness. For this very reason, we have to bring shame into the light so that God can bring forgiveness of sins and release of judgement.

Can you remember when you were little, as you lay in bed at night trying to sleep, you would look at something in your room and believe it was a monster or some strange figure watching you? Then when you put the light on, you realized that it was only a jacket hanging from the cupboard door, or your dirty laundry from the day in the corner of your bedroom. The monster only lives in the dark and only you can see it, but the truth of its identity can only be exposed once God's light shines upon it.

> *"A sound heart is the life of the flesh: but envy the rottenness of the bones"* (Proverbs 14:30).

> *"When swelling and pride come, then emptiness and shame come also..."* (Proverbs 11:2).

> *"Don't be afraid, for you won't be ashamed; don't be discouraged, for you won't be disgraced. You will forget the shame of your youth, no longer remember the dishonour of being widowed"* (Isaiah 54:4).

It is so vital that we confess our shame and, if we can, the issues which caused the shame in our lives, to someone. Be very selective to choose someone trustworthy who has empathy and understanding, someone who is not judgemental, someone with integrity who can speak the truth in love. If you pick someone untrustworthy, it can lead to more shame and emotional wounding.

"Confess to one another therefore your faults (your slips, false steps, your offenses, your sins) and pray also for one another, that you may be healed and restored [to a spiritual tone of mind and heart]" (James 5:16).

> *"You know how I am insulted, shamed and disgraced; before you stand all my foes"* (Psalm 69:19).

God knows all about your shame, who and what caused it and how to be free from it. It takes courage and a willingness to be vulnerable before Him in order to exchange your shame for what He has for you.

The opposite of shame is honour. When we are cleansed, we do not have to carry dishonour or shame, but we can lift our heads and fix our gaze on Him to see the image which He is reflecting back at us. Now we can discover our true identity and not carry the shame of the past.

Loved and nurtured people experience Godly fruit in their relationships.

FRUIT:

Peace, joy, mercy
Kind, patient, gentle
Acceptance, ghenerosity, purity, trust, integrity

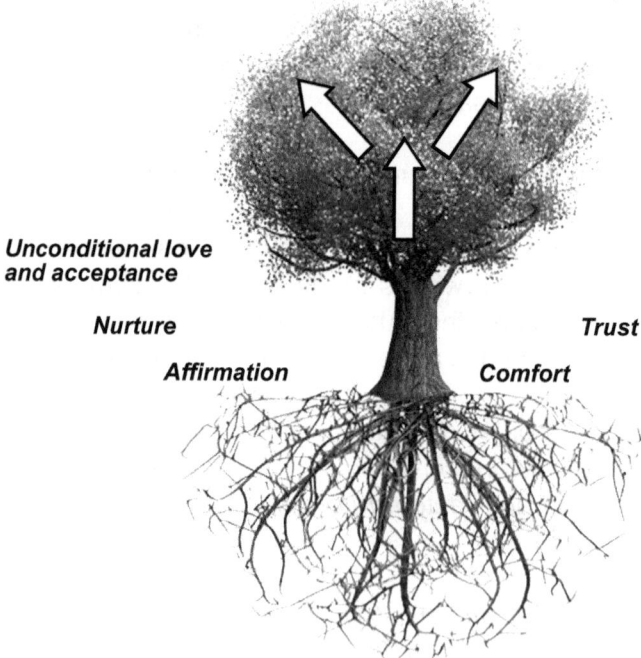

Unconditional love and acceptance

Nurture

Trust

Affirmation

Comfort

Distortions in our relationships produce negative fruit.

FRUIT:
Fear, sadness, conflict, isolation,
Unlovingness, cruelty, striving, shame, guilt
Harshness, jealousy, envy
Lack of trust and generosity, defilement, disorder, disease

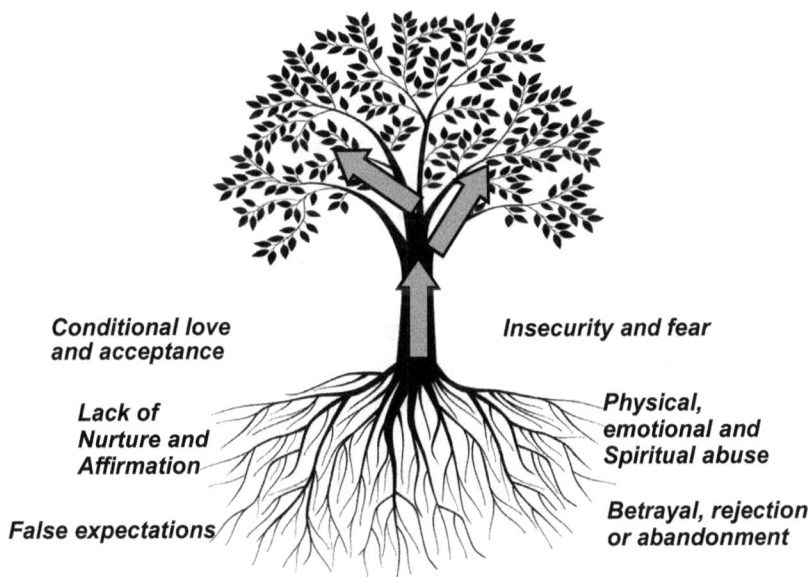

Conditional love and acceptance

Insecurity and fear

Lack of Nurture and Affirmation

Physical, emotional and Spiritual abuse

False expectations

Betrayal, rejection or abandonment

To have an even clearer understanding, I would like to use specific examples of real life situations where physical, psychological and spiritual disorder and brokenness can occur:

Case Study:

Esther grew up as an only child and was cherished by both her parents. She had a very close bond with her dad. However, when she was six years old, her dad had a sudden heart attack and passed away. Her mom told her that there was no need to cry because her dad is with Jesus. Her bond with her mom grew stronger and she always worried about what would happen if her mom were to die too. Her mom remarried three years later (when Esther was nine years old) to a man who had a twelve-year-old son. Esther never felt that she belonged in this new family setting. She tried very hard to please her stepdad by doing things for him in the hope that he would notice her. She felt that she always had to compete for his attention because of her new stepbrother. At the same time, she was very resentful towards her new dad and brother because she had to share her mom with them.

Many years later, after completing her studies (BCom), Esther met Paul and they soon got married. Both Esther and Paul are Christians. They had three children and Esther decided to stay home to home-school their children. Esther was a perfectionist and always very well organized. She was a very loving mother to her children though. Paul became a very successful businessman and travelled often. While he was away on a business trip, there was a burglary while Esther and the children were at home. She was held at gunpoint in her bedroom while the children were fortunately still sleeping. Although they did not experience any physical harm, she was very traumatized by this incident. She suffered from anxiety and was very fearful every time Paul had to go away. She internalized the fear and the anxiety because she did not want to upset the children. Paul was not very supportive during this whole time because he was very distant when he was home; also, Esther made out to be fine.

Eighteen months after the burglary, Paul came home one evening and told Esther that he is filing for a divorce. He moved out of the home two days later to leave for New Zealand where he started a new job. Esther was devastated because she never expected him to be unfaithful, let alone move to a different country. Being alone with the children and struggling to be there for them created even more anxiety. She had to find a school for the kids and find a job after not having worked for so many years. Disciplining the children was difficult and she felt sorry for them because of the fact that Paul had abandoned them. She often lashed out at the kids when they did something wrong and afterwards she felt so guilty about her

The progression and the physical effects of fear and anxiety caused by unresolved trauma in Esther's life.

Traumatic experience in early childhood.
Body releases hormones to deal with shock and trauma.

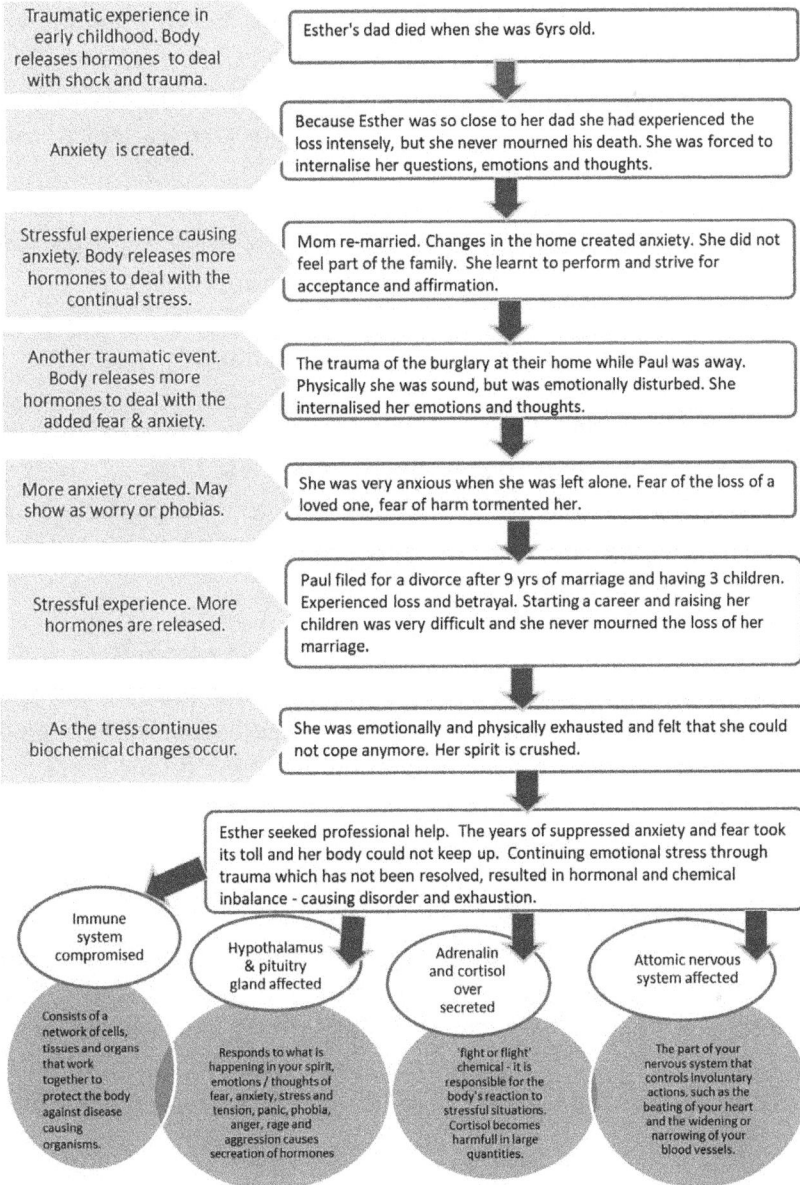

Traumatic experience in early childhood. Body releases hormones to deal with shock and trauma.	Esther's dad died when she was 6yrs old.
Anxiety is created.	Because Esther was so close to her dad she had experienced the loss intensely, but she never mourned his death. She was forced to internalise her questions, emotions and thoughts.
Stressful experience causing anxiety. Body releases more hormones to deal with the continual stress.	Mom re-married. Changes in the home created anxiety. She did not feel part of the family. She learnt to perform and strive for acceptance and affirmation.
Another traumatic event. Body releases more hormones to deal with the added fear & anxiety.	The trauma of the burglary at their home while Paul was away. Physically she was sound, but was emotionally disturbed. She internalised her emotions and thoughts.
More anxiety created. May show as worry or phobias.	She was very anxious when she was left alone. Fear of the loss of a loved one, fear of harm tormented her.
Stressful experience. More hormones are released.	Paul filed for a divorce after 9 yrs of marriage and having 3 children. Experienced loss and betrayal. Starting a career and raising her children was very difficult and she never mourned the loss of her marriage.
As the tress continues biochemical changes occur.	She was emotionally and physically exhausted and felt that she could not cope anymore. Her spirit is crushed.

Esther seeked professional help. The years of suppressed anxiety and fear took its toll and her body could not keep up. Continuing emotional stress through trauma which has not been resolved, resulted in hormonal and chemical inbalance - causing disorder and exhaustion.

Immune system compromised
Consists of a network of cells, tissues and organs that work together to protect the body against disease causing organisms.

Hypothalamus & pituitry gland affected
Responds to what is happening in your spirit, emotions / thoughts of fear, anxiety, stress and tension, panic, phobia, anger, rage and aggression causes secreation of hormones

Adrenalin and cortisol over secreted
'fight or flight' chemical - it is responsible for the body's reaction to stressful situations. Cortisol becomes harmfull in large quantities.

Attomic nervous system affected
The part of your nervous system that controls involuntary actions, such as the beating of your heart and the widening or narrowing of your blood vessels.

reactions and the anxiety she has instilled in them because of this. Although Paul sent money towards the children's education each month, the financial and emotional pressure took its toll on Esther. It brought her to a place of depression and physical exhaustion and she found it very difficult to cope with normal day-to-day duties and expectations. She suffered from chronic tension headaches, stomach ulcers, eczema and chronic viral and bacterial infections. She often visited her general practitioner until she was referred to somebody for professional counselling and was diagnosed with depression and severe exhaustion.

NB: See previous page with diagram of how Esther's life started well as a little baby, but ended in depression.

Consequences of the trauma in Esther's life:

Internalizing and dissociating from her true emotions: Since the time her dad died, she learnt that she doesn't have to express emotions, so she was a strong girl and only believed the facts. After the burglary, she struggled with fear and anxiety, but tried to be strong for the kids and acted 'fine'.

Deep sense of loss and unresolved grief in her spirit:
Loss of her dad (she was still longing for her dad as a little girl) – she never mourned the loss of her dad; loss of her sense of belonging (in her family); loss of her peace (after the burglary); loss of her marriage; loss of her self-worth as a wife (woman) because of the betrayal.

Fear and anxiety:
Fear of the loss of loved ones; fear of rejection in the new family; fear of failure and rejection with her stepdad (if she did not perform or succeed in something, she would not be noticed); fear of being harmed after the break-in; fear of being alone; fear of not being able to provide for her children after Paul left.

All of the above created constant continuous anxiety/stress which became a lifestyle.

Guilt:
She could never do enough to win the affection of her stepdad and developed a low self-esteem.
She felt guilty when Paul divorced her – she always wondered what she could have done differently or done more or done less to have saved her marriage.
She felt guilty about the way she lashed out at the children when she was under pressure.
She felt guilty that the children did not have a mom and a dad and felt very sorry for them; this made disciplining very difficult and created more anxiety.

Shame:
She was ashamed about being known as a divorced woman.
She was ashamed about not being 'strong' enough and not being able to cope with her situation.
She felt that she had failed her children, herself and God.

The inability to deal with the trauma created core beliefs (mostly perceived) in her spirit from a very young age. Based on these beliefs, she made decisions and reacted accordingly for the rest of her life – until God could bring correction and wholeness.

Physical disease/disorder caused by Esther's emotional and spiritual journey:

Monophobia (Fear of being alone/fear of solitude) – caused by the traumatic break-in at her home – unresolved fear and anxiety.

Chronic headaches – caused by constant fear, anxiety and stress in her thought life. The tension leads to muscle spasms in the neck, forehead and jaw.

Stomach ulcer – When the immune system is weakened due to high levels of stress hormones (over a long period of time), it has little defence against the helicobacter pylori bacteria which infect the stomach lining resulting in inflammation. There is also an increase in the production of stomach acid and a prevention of the growth of the stomach lining. This all results in the forming of an ulcer.

Eczema – involves itching, redness and inflammation of the skin. It is a fear, anxiety and stress disorder resulting in excessive histamine secretion. Histamine is a chemical found in some of the body's cells. When stressed, the immune system mistakenly believes that certain substances e.g. food, dust etc. is harmful to the body. In attempt to protect the body, the immune system starts a chain reaction that prompts the release of histamine. The skin, eyes, nose, throat, lungs and gastrointestinal tract react to oversecretion of histamine.

Chronic viral or bacterial infections – When the immune system is compromised and weakened due to ongoing oversecretion of stress hormones, the cells of the immune system, which are responsible for detecting and killing harmful cells, are damaged. It is therefore easy for bacteria, viruses and fungi to attack the body cells and cause infections, inflammation and disease.

Depression and physical exhaustion – a result of conflict in the human spirit and on a soul level which the hypothalamus (limbic system) responds to, causing an imbalance in chemical and hormonal secretions. Esther is experiencing fatigue and exhaustion due to the long-term fear, anxiety and stress which can cause a depletion in the body's potassium levels. Potassium helps the cells in the body eliminate toxic waste, promotes balanced pH levels and increases energy. The body is simply saying "Time-out!"

Esther has learned and owned the habit of anxiety and stress and she has allowed the spirit of fear (demonic) to torment her.

Esther has reached a crossroad in her life where she has to make free will choices. She has to choose if she will give every area of her life to a Loving Heavenly Father. Will she allow Him to bring healing to every part of her being where there is physical, emotional and spiritual pain and brokenness? In the same way Esther has to make a choice, you too have to make that same choice. It is a choice that will impact your life dramatically and will determine whether you will walk in your God-given destiny or not. God has come to give abundant life, but the enemy has come to steal, kill and destroy.

> *"The thief's purpose is to steal and kill and destroy.*
> *My purpose is to give them a rich and satisfying life"*
> (John 10:10).

Brokenness and damage can occur in your body, in your soul and in your spirit. According to Scripture – what happens in our spirit determines what we think, how we feel emotionally and how we act or react accordingly in a physical manner. Brokenness in our spirit causes emotional breakdown and physical disease. Disease and disorder are not just random events. You do not wake up one morning and suddenly you have depression, or OCD (obsessive compulsive disorder).

Disease and brokenness are not from God!

Managing the symptoms through medication and isolating people must be seen as temporary – a bridge between disease/brokenness and wholeness. We have to deal with the cause and the effect of disease/brokenness. God (and the principles of His Word) is the solution. Healing is God's mercy. He wants to heal so that we can be who He created us to be. Healing and wholeness are our birthright!

"I long, yes, I faint with longing to enter the courts of the Lord. With my whole being, body and soul, I will shout joyfully to the living God" (Psalm 84:2).

Chapter 4

Parts of Me

In this chapter, I would like to take you a step further and show you some of the implications of trauma, and specifically childhood trauma (abuse), and the impact they have on every part of a human being.

Let us first define what trauma is.

The word 'trauma' means 'wounding'. Wounding can obviously take place on a physical level – trauma to the physical body. You can also experience trauma on an emotional and psychological level. Emotional and psychological trauma are the result of extraordinarily stressful events that shatter your sense of security, making you feel helpless in a dangerous situation. Traumatic experiences often involve a threat to life or safety, but any situation that leaves you feeling overwhelmed and isolated can be traumatic, even if it doesn't involve physical harm. Trauma is an event that combines fear and terror with actual or perceived lack of control. It is a life-changing experience with negative consequences – often lifelong. What is traumatic to one person may not be traumatic to another, because what one person sees as fearful, overwhelming or painful may not be so for somebody else. Experiencing trauma in childhood can have a severe and long-lasting effect. When childhood trauma is not resolved, a sense of fear and helplessness carries over into adulthood, setting the stage for further trauma.

Childhood trauma can result from anything that disrupts a child's sense of safety, including: an unstable or unsafe environment, separation from a parent, serious/chronic illness, intrusive medical procedures, sexual, physical or verbal abuse, domestic violence or neglect.

Let us delve a bit deeper into the consequences of childhood trauma. I want to focus on sexual abuse/molestation and show you what happens in the body, the soul and in the spirit of such a child – every created part of the child – how it cripples them and how they become adults with deep brokenness, fragmented personalities, living a sinful life and not knowing who they really are. These facts are firstly based on what I have personally experienced from childhood to adulthood; Secondly, knowledge I have gained through many years of formal and informal studies in the area of healing, deliverance and wholeness; and thirdly, through working with people who have suffered childhood trauma.

Definition of sexual abuse:

The violation of physical boundaries and free will, where actions of any sexual nature are involved. It is usually undesired sexual behaviour by one person upon another. This can also include undressing a person (through intimidation and instilling fear) and using him/her in photoshoots/films for sexual stimulation or pornography. The term also covers any behaviour by an adult or older adolescent towards a child to stimulate any of the involved sexually. It can be an older person engaging in indecent exposure (of the genitals, female nipples, etc.) to a child with intent to gratify their own sexual desires or to intimidate or groom the child. Child grooming is befriending and establishing an emotional connection with a child, and sometimes the family, to lower the child's inhibitions with the object of sexual abuse. The use of a child, or other individuals younger than the age of consent, for sexual stimulation is referred to as child sexual abuse or statutory rape. When force is immediate, of short duration or infrequent, it is called sexual assault.

Where does sexual abuse usually take place and who are the abusers?

In a World Health Organization study, 47.6% of young women and 31.9% of young men claimed that their first intercourse was forced or somewhat coerced by family members or persons known to their family. Children are often sexually abused by somebody familiar; someone they know and trust; someone who is actually supposed to protect them, instead of violating, defiling and using them, e.g. a teacher, brother, father, uncle, mother, sister, family friend etc.

Often there is a social tolerance and acceptance of child sexual abuse because of stigma, fear and sometimes lack of trust in authorities. In many cases, a non-abusive parent remains silent and is reluctant to file charges against the perpetrator. There is a high percentage of the non-abusive partners who turn a 'blind eye' when children are sexually abused in their family. The abuser will always look for opportunities to take advantage of and will even create opportunities in order to isolate the child they prey upon. The child will often be offered a 'reward' if they 'play along' and fear will always be instilled in order to keep the secret. The abuser will, for instance, say to the child, "If you share our secret, they will not believe you and they will send you away" or "If you tell anybody, I will ...". This not only creates confusion emotionally, but also sexually in the mind of a child. The child receives 'attention', 'comfort', 'love' and maybe even gifts, yet they are confused because this type of 'attention' or 'love' does not feel right. It feels wrong, defiling and overwhelming. A child forms a perverted perception of what love, attention and affirmation is. The confusion and fear keep the child in a place of submission to do as they are told by the abuser.

The offender is referred to as a sexual abuser or molester. Child sexual abuse offenders are not always paedophiles unless they have a primary or exclusive sexual interest in prepubescent children and act on it. In other words, a child sexual abuser or molester is someone who has acted on sexual desires – this can be indecent exposure, touching/petting or rape. A paedophile is a person who has a sexual interest in children under the age of 13 years – he has sexual desires or fantasies to physically molest/rape a child, but does not act on those desires (yet). Paedophiles are frequently uncomfortable with adult intimacy and may spend their lives manoeuvring to be near children. They may be extremely charming and skilled at manipulating adults and they may use adult relationships to gain access to children.

Terminology can be misleading and confusing. So many times, I have heard people say "Well, at least it was only touching and no penetration." The fact is that whether it is inappropriate touching or rape, it is traumatic to the child and brings immense harm to their identity and security. It should never be brushed off as 'not that bad' – it is never acceptable and never 'ok' for any child to endure such injustice!

Child sexual abuse also often runs in family lines (generations) and I have often seen that it can be families who are either involved with or descendants of Free Masons, because of the sexual rituals, perversions and acts of lust in the lodges.

It can present itself as:
- Generational sexual abuse (incest) – Children can be exposed to sexual acts and perversion amongst various family members or it can be one specific family member who will act as the abuser. This can also happen in a ritualistic way, as it can be daily, at certain times or in certain situations. Like brushing your teeth or eating, it becomes a ritual/habit. This results in serious long-term psychological trauma especially if the abuser is a parental figure.

- Satanic ritual abuse is sexual acts during rituals where children are purposefully abused which are normally more violent and perverse in nature. Children born in active occultic families can be exposed to both generational and ritual abuse. They can be abused at home and be part of sex orgies, sacrifices and rituals when the cult expect them to be involved. We will look more at the spiritual influence and attachments of this in Chapter 6.

This level of abuse leads to complex trauma. Complex trauma means that the child who was supposed to be protected (kept safe), nurtured and loved unconditionally by the people who were fulfilling this vital role of authority, were exposed, used, abused, neglected and even tormented by these people. As adults, these victims develop multiple disorders and disease due to the constant and repetitive trauma they were exposed to over long periods of time.

If you become aware that sexual abuse has occurred, ensure that the child gets the support that he/she needs. It is a criminal offence that has to be reported. Often a child will need to work with a therapist to recover from what has happened. Unfortunately, children won't just recover from sexual abuse on their own. They will need help to process what has happened and develop healthy responses to their experiences and surroundings. Even if a child seems fine, you should still seek out professional help. It takes a huge amount of courage for a child to break the silence, so if they do spill the beans, never react in disbelief. They need to know that you have their backs, that they are safe with you and that you actually do believe them. Young children usually do not make up stories of a sexual nature unless they have been exposed to a sexual act.

The physical response of the body and the soul to sexual abuse

Our brains have lots of independent parts that need to work together in order to help us process our surroundings and have healthy, productive responses. Two of the most important parts of the brain are the limbic system and the prefrontal cortex. The limbic system is the survival part of our brain. It drives us toward safety by avoiding pain and seeking pleasure. These drives are powerful and occur mostly on a subconscious level. In contrast to the limbic system, the prefrontal cortex is the rational, conscious part of our brain where logical reasoning, abstract thinking and behaviour regulation occur.

From infancy, the brain is in an immense learning phase as we experience the world around us, and our brains continue to develop for many years until we reach the age of 25. If trauma from sexual abuse occurs during childhood and teen years, the brain's development can be influenced and scared. The limbic system can get stuck in a never-ending survival mode and see the world as an unsafe place even after threats of danger fade. The instinctual limbic system will overpower the rational prefrontal cortex and make a child feel unsafe constantly, whether there's something to be afraid of or not.

In young children or teenagers, the prefrontal cortex is not yet developed which means that they do not have the ability to:

- *Focus on one thing while ignoring distractions* – they get distracted easily.
- *Make good, logical decisions* – Behaviour is based on emotions rather than logic. This means that children do not rationalize and do not have the ability to solve problems. They also cannot assess risky or dangerous situations logically. They feel. The emotions are reality.
- *Develop their personalities* – This is because of traumatic environmental input and overstimulation.
- *Remember detail of the memory* – The prefrontal cortex plays a crucial role in integrating the information (data) from the child's surroundings to form a memory (a story of what happened). The prefrontal cortex is still developing and now has to cope with a traumatic event. Children who are abused at a young age can even suffer with memory restrictions when they reach adulthood.

When there is danger or a perceived threat to survival, the central nervous system activates the 'fight', 'flight' or 'freeze' response.

When this response is activated, there is a dramatic increase in stress hormones released to create a hyperarousal (hyperalert) state. The body is now prepared to fight or run from the danger.

When fleeing or fighting is impossible, the body is prepared to freeze through dissociation.

- The victim feels numb and disengaged.
- The victim may faint.
- Time is suspended (they lose track of time; five minutes can feel like an hour or the other way around).
- Derealization or depersonalization may occur – an alteration in the perception or experience of 'self' or the external world so that it seems unreal. This is a form of dissociation. To increase the chance of survival, the victim complies with the abuser, 'submitting' under the abuse. Once a child learns any type of dissociation in order to feel 'safer', they can continue to do so into adulthood.

Trauma changes not only how children think and what they think about, but also their very capacity to think.

The problem comes when this 'fight', 'flight' or 'freeze' response is stimulated too often. Harmful effects occur to the body. The stress response is triggered the same by both physical and emotional pain. So, whether there is actual physical danger or the danger is perceived, you will be in a constant fight-or-flight state. The long-term oversecretion of stress hormones cause serious damage to the individual's brain development, mind/memory and health.

If a child is exposed to significant stress during the first three years of life, full development of facial expression of feelings, perception of emotion and regulation of the nervous system will be affected.

Children who have been exposed to prolonged trauma may have more sensitive and intense responses to all stress. E.g. They would be more sensitive or irritable with loud noises, strong odours or flashes of light etc. – any trigger that stimulates the 'fight' or 'flight' response. Each time the child is stressed again, the sensitivity of the response is increased and makes the child more vulnerable to anxiety disorders and depression.

To an adult who can think logically and assess danger, an abusive situation/rape will be extremely overwhelming. Can you imagine what a little five-year-old child must feel? Even one incident is too much.

One lady (in her 50's) came to see me after losing two close family members in a short period of time to cancer (trauma). She is a very sensitive, caring person. She grew up in a very loving home with both parents. During the conversation, she spoke about some fear issues she had and responded, "Oh, I am just a fearful person. I have always been like that." I asked her to pray about it because God never created her to be a fearful person – it is contrary to who He is and we have been created in His likeness. Long story short, when she was six years old, she was playing in the garden of their home. Her dad was in the house. Their gardener (who was very familiar) approached her and started to pull her underwear down. Before he could physically touch her, her father came out into the garden and saw what was happening. He came to her rescue before the gardener 'harmed' her. She could not make sense of it at that age and went into a 'freeze' state. She explained that she just stood there and did not know what to do. The fact is, the defilement, fear and confusion overwhelmed her and made her fearful all her life, until she actually dealt with the trauma of that incident and God set her free.

Memory of emotions, sounds, smells, touches and tastes is recorded on cellular level. Remember the information-emotion molecules in the bloodstream bind to the receptors of the body cells and carry a copy of the memory and the emotion linked to a specific thought/memory.

Survivors of traumatic events and abuse may have been too young or to overwhelmed by the trauma to remember the event, often blocked out of the memory in the brain (dissociation). Yet, your body remembers. Survivors of traumatic abuse will often experience aches and pains which manifest in the physical body – even years after the incident, but cannot be medically diagnosed; or when something triggers that memory (on cellular level not in the brain) they can even experience symptoms of an illness/disorder which they have had as a child during the period of abuse. As an example, I had the privilege of ministering to a lady who was severely abused by a close family friend over many years. As she was dealing with the trauma as an adult, she suddenly developed psoriasis. In asking whether she had had it before, she realized that she had it periodically as a little girl – during the time she was exposed to the abuse. Psoriasis is an anxiety disorder of the skin. Some women (very happily married) complain of irregular intense abdominal and vaginal pain just before intimacy with their husbands. This is because of the cellular memory of the physical pain experienced during rape, even many years earlier. A survivor of sexual abuse who has overcome and is healed from the abuse sometimes thinks he/she has moved on, yet they still struggle in some areas because they have dealt with memories in the brain and emotional pain, but they have not dealt with body memory which was experienced on a cellular level.

Effects of child sexual abuse can include the following:

Dissociation:

When your mind has resolved itself to the idea that it can neither fight nor flee, it will freeze. Your body will begin to secrete endorphins which will help numb you to the pain of the moment in order to survive the attack. You will dissociate from what is happening in the moment. Your mind goes someplace else and it is as if the trauma is not really happening to you.

Depersonalization and derealization are types of dissociation which are common among victims of abuse. Depersonalization is when the victim disconnects from 'self' on a physical and emotional level. They feel like they are having an out-of-body experience. They feel dead, disconnected, and as if their head is not attached to their body. Some will say that they feel spaced out or drugged and this feeling will come and go. They might feel robotic – going through the day and doing stuff but not registering or remembering. They do not remember very well because they do not feel present all the time. They will look in the mirror and, in their head, they will know it is them they are looking at, but they feel as if it is somebody else looking back at them. They feel disconnected from the image they see. They have a problem with tangibility – they can look at their hands and feel they are not theirs, yet they can feel their fingers rubbing against each other.

Derealization is when the victim is disconnected from the environment. A person might say that she cannot see enough or can't open her eyes wide enough; the environment (room) is either too bright or too dark. Colours can be sharp and heavily outlined (like in comic books) or colours can appear muted and blend together. Vision can be distorted and change from micro (everything around you is enlarged and you are tiny) or macro (you feel too big for the room). Surroundings can look distorted and altered where, for example, the ground you're standing on or the walls of the room move – in wavy or breathing motion.

These two forms of dissociation can be experienced at the same time or interchangeably and is not substance (drug) related. The person is not on a 'high' due to medication, alcohol or drugs.

Repressed memories or memory loss:

Many adult survivors of traumatic abuse and experiences suffer from memory loss. Although many trauma survivors are able to remember how they felt when they were children, they do not always remember why they felt or feel the way they do today. They may feel like they were abused, but they might not remember precisely why they feel that way. Some people might say that they know deep down that something bad happened to them, but they have no memory of the actual abuse. The brain under stress has a difficult time recalling vivid memories related to specific traumas. It is very common for abused adult children to suffer from memory loss related to traumatic experiences. When the brain is put on high alert due to a traumatic experience, the adrenal glands secrete cortisol readying the victim to fight or flee. What people don't usually think about is the third panic response which is called 'the freeze response'. Children are TOTALLY powerless to their abusers and they can neither flee nor fight, so what they do then is freeze. And this is not their fault.

When the brain understands it cannot get away from an abuser or abusive situation, the brain floods with cortisol. When this happens under extreme stress, the cortisol hijacks the hippocampus. The hippocampus is the area of the brain that is responsible for 'cataloguing memories'. The amygdala will alert the brain that danger is near and it is the hippocampus that will file all the data associated with the danger within the brain for later use. Cataloguing events enables the brain to recall 'stories' of events later when needed. But, when it comes to powerless children who are living with their abusers or sent to be taken care of by their abusers and alike, collected data is not stored the way it should be and is useless because children are powerless – making the recall of the event very difficult and even impossible.

When the mind has presumed it cannot fight or flee from an attack, the brain can become so overwhelmed with analgesic type chemicals, the body is saved from physical pain. In the case of small children, having the hippocampus overwhelmed can help prevent a child from splitting psychologically and enabling the child to survive the trauma. Sexual abuse can cause a child to feel insane or suffer psychotic breaks.

Flashbacks/Nightmares

Flashbacks:
These are when you are 'pulled' into a traumatic event – meaning in your mind it feels like you are back in that time/space when it physically happened to you. It is almost like you are not there in the flesh but you experience the whole event through your five senses all over again. This is usually due to triggers. It could be that you hear a certain word or someone's voice, smell a specific smell or see somebody with specific characteristics which are similar or the same as when the abuse took place. People often say that it just happened suddenly or that it just came out of nowhere. This is due to the fact that our bodies respond on a cellular level without our minds even knowing what is happening. We are not always consciously aware which of the five senses triggered it.

We have two types of memory. One is a non-traumatic memory which will be memories of normal day to day events and experiences such as going to the beach or a day at the office. Nothing scary happens, you do not fear for your life or someone else's life and you are just having a good time. Your brain forms a story about your trip to the beach and gets stored on the nerve cells in your mind; your cortex, amygdale and hippocampus are involved in this process. It is easy for you to recall detail about your trip to the beach in the order things happened later on when you want to tell somebody about the lovely morning you had.

On the other hand, you could also have traumatic memory which is very different from non-traumatic memory. Traumatic memory occurs when you are going about your day as usual and you encounter something which overwhelms you, something that is so scary and so painful, that your brain cannot process it. It happens too fast and it is too overwhelming and you go into a 'freeze' state. Your brain cannot form a 'story' with detail of what is happening as it is supposed to (like when you went to the beach). Bits and pieces of what the five senses can pick up are recorded, such as:

You smelled a specific smell; there were pine trees; the perpetrator had a green shirt on or the overwhelming feeling of terror and pain. Everything is muddled up in your brain and there is no logical sequence of events. These memories are not stored orderly and in the right place on the nerve cells in your memory like a non-traumatic memory. These bits and pieces flood other nerve cells where other non-traumatic memory is stored.

Flashbacks happen when you go about your day and you have to recall a non-traumatic memory; you suddenly smell something similar or see somebody with a green shirt near a pine forest... and boom! With that recalled memory, you have one or more of the bits and pieces (that went everywhere during the traumatic incident) which triggers the trauma again. That is why you feel that it just comes out of nowhere.

If these flashbacks are ignored and not dealt with, they can get worse, carry on for longer and happen more frequently. The flashback can trigger all the emotions, fears, feelings of helplessness etc. which can make it a very traumatic experience in itself.

Nightmares:
Children who have experienced sexual assault often have nightmares every night, sometimes more than once. They may have recurring dreams which are all the more frightening because they know what is coming. Nightmares can make children terrified of the dark and bedtime, leading to difficult behaviours. Their dreams are reflecting their fears and their sense of lack of control. Looking at the content of their dreams can help them to talk about what has happened.

Shame:
There is a very defiling aspect that sexual abuse brings into a child's life. It is not only a feeling that makes them feel like a bad person (as discussed previously), but also a feeling that makes them feel dirty and used on a very deep level.

Guilt/Self-blame:

Children assume they are at fault when Mommy and Daddy (or somebody who is supposed to care and protect them) abuse them. When the child assumes responsibility for the abuse, the traumatic events make sense to the child's innocent mind. They may think, "Daddy did this to me because I am bad." Although it is an inappropriate thought, it is a thought that helps the child make sense out of a situation they are not physically in control over. Sometimes the abuser will actually reinforce this belief by telling the child that he is doing it because the child is naughty or did something bad. There is another safety precaution that gets to be addressed in this type of thinking as well. If a child is responsible for being abused, then on some level the child will feel that he/she can stop the abuse. The thinking sounds something like, "If I started it, I can stop it and one day I will figure out just how to do that." This form of thinking offers the child a much-needed sense of hope as well as control over their dire circumstances.

Children who are stuck in repetitive trauma over their lifetimes may not always remember their traumas. When trauma and stress are the norm, events become blurred. Nothing that happens seems 'out of the ordinary'. Abuse and neglect are the norm. If nobody (adults or authorities) 'act like' what you are going through is abusive, it is difficult, if not impossible, to acknowledge that what you are going through is abusive. If abuse is the norm, then your experience is the norm and does not seem abnormal.

Children who are being abused need a witness. They need an adult from the outside to acknowledge for them that what they are going through is inappropriate and not their fault. Otherwise, children will assume everything that is happening is their fault and, because abuse is 'the norm', they will not be able to identify the fact that what they have suffered was in fact abuse. When this is the case, abused adult children stay below the veil of consciousness, believe everything that is going wrong in their life is their fault, suffer from low self-worth, become addicted, and attract abusive partners as well as friends. Without awareness, the cycles of abuse continue.

Fear and anxiety:
When children are not physically, emotionally or spiritually protected or cared for, they become insecure and grow up with constant anxiety. This type of fear is deeply rooted and affects the whole of the person's being. Almost all survivors of childhood abuse will acknowledge that, deep down, they have never felt safe or they have never trusted anybody. They have grown up with the fear and anxiety of always wondering when the 'next time' will be, who knows about it, what will happen if somebody finds out, etc. Fear is progressive and will result in fear of man, fear of punishment, fear of pain (getting hurt), fear of rejection, fear of authoritative figures, fear of trusting people, fear of intimacy, and the list goes on. Women sometimes fear the fact that men might find them attractive, so they will neglect themselves or become obese to avoid becoming a victim again. In previous chapters, we have discussed other consequences of how long-term fear and anxiety affects the body.

Learning difficulties:
The negative effect that the stress hormones have on the brain and memory can create much difficulty for a child even going into adulthood when it comes to learning and remembering what they have learned. They can find it hard to keep their attention (focus) on one thing for a long period. Children may also develop speech problems, e.g. stuttering, as a result of the constant fear, anxiety and insecurity, causing difficulty at school level (making friends or bullying). This can lead to more anxiety and more difficulty with memory and improving a healthy self-esteem.

On the other hand, children may become intensely focused on schoolwork to the exclusion of other activities in an effort to cope. This is fantastic for their report cards and grades, but is in fact just another way of dissociating from the trauma in order to get through each day by keeping busy. Some children will excel in their school work up to a certain age and suddenly turn around and have absolutely no interest in studying or achieving anything at school.

Behavioural problems:

Lack of critical nurturing and exposure to traumatic stress and abuse alters the nervous system, predisposing the child to be impulsive, overreactive and violent. The fact that the child cannot reason or make any logical sense of what happened to them – the confusion and frustration, the deep sense and knowing of injustice and the emotional/physical pain they have to endure while keeping the 'secret' is a recipe for disaster and destruction. It is like a pressure cooker waiting to explode. They have no way to express what is going on, on the inside, and it will manifest in their behaviour – 'screaming' for help and attention in the only way they know how to. Their lack of control over the abuse may make them feel that their future is unsure, which can lead some children to act recklessly. They may engage in reckless play. Where the preschool child will crash their truck a hundred times into a wall, the school age child might physically engage in dangerous games as a way of exercising a sense of control that was lost during the abuse. Some children might have emotional outbursts or rage. Often children might undress themselves while screaming and either curl up into a foetal position or hide somewhere where they feel safe. The sad reality is that some of these children are then labelled as the 'naughty' or 'bad' child which only reinforces the negative belief system that already exists.

Bedwetting:

Many young children lose bladder/bowel control following sexual assault. It can be frustrating for parents and cause extra work. It can be humiliating and embarrassing for children. It is easy for adults and children to focus on the consequences of wetting and soiling, e.g. changing sheets/clothes and washing, rather than the reasons why it happens.

All children bed-wet from time to time when they are sick, stressed or anxious. Children who have been sexually assaulted will often bed-wet every night and sometimes more than once a night. Bed-wetting can be linked to feelings and may be a result of nightmares.

Bed-wetting can also result from feelings of helplessness when children feel a loss of ownership and power over their body when it has been used by someone more powerful than they are. Bed-wetting can be a reflection of children regressing in many ways, following sexual assault, when they lose a number of skills they previously had. Children may regress to a younger state to try and get their needs met. Bed-wetting and soiling may also occur because a child separates from his/her genital/urinary/anal areas. They may lose the ability to respond to their body cues and therefore become less able to regulate their toilet habits. Sometimes children may be scared to actually go to the toilet. They may have experienced sexual assault in a bathroom or their fears may focus on the toilet itself.

Sexual dysfunction and perversion:
When children are sexually assaulted, their sense of what is right and wrong becomes distorted. Whatever they had previously learnt about bodies and sexual activity becomes invalid. If a child was shown how to light a fire, for example, it is likely that the child will attempt to repeat what they saw. If children have learnt that they get attention by being sexual with one person, they may well repeat the behaviour with another person. If children have experienced sexual feelings, which are common in children who have been sexually assaulted, they are likely to try and recreate those reactions. The brain releases hormones that not only stimulate and satisfy, but makes them feel good.

Children have learnt that sexual activity should be hidden and they may start to masturbate secretly at a very young age. They may begin to sexually act out with other children to try and make sense of what has happened to them. Their curiosity about sexual matters may have been activated years before they develop the intellectual ability to understand. Children may want to sexually act out on other children to make them feel less vulnerable or, in the same way, they may be aggressive. The trouble they may get into as a result of this behaviour then confirms their view of themselves as dirty and bad. Sexual acting out usually involves a difference in power between the children and may involve coercion/force or blackmail and a repetition of an adult sexual activity which they have experienced. Early adolescents will masturbate and begin to develop relationships that involve a range of touching.

Sexual acting out in children who have been assaulted will involve either the child repeating what has been done to them on other children or getting other children to do to them what the offender did. It can also involve children approaching adults in a sexual way. It does not mean that the child automatically becomes an offender but it is an indication that professional help is needed.

During the teenage years and adulthood, women might believe that they are only good for what they can offer men on a sexual level and this factor often drives them into prostitution or fornication – going from one man to the next. As a child, they might have been exposed to various perverted sexual practices and grow up thinking it is 'ok', e.g. pornography, multiple sexual partners, same sex partners, masturbation, bestiality (sexual acts with animals) etc.

According to psychology, sexual activity between children is about exploration and can be quite 'normal' for them to masturbate. Sexual, perverted acts by children or teens needs to be distinct from what is normal according to what God says about the body and sex and not what psychology suggests. When children are acting out on a sexual level or becoming sexually active prematurely, the alarms and red lights should be going off!

Chronic pelvic pain and other physical pain:
Lots of children develop aches and pains that have no physical cause. These will often have a connection to an aspect of the assault. Sometimes, if a child has experienced physical pain during the assaults, their body can retain the memory of this pain (remember body memories and the information-emotion-molecules attached to the cells of your body?). Pelvic or vaginal pains may be experienced because of forced penetration. Severe headaches can

be as a result of either the overwhelming anxiety or physical abuse that accompanied the sexual abuse. These aches and pains can come and go as the child grows or only appear later in adulthood. Children may also think that something is broken inside of them. Repeated pain can also be a way for children to gain the extra love and attention they need at the time. Sometimes emotions manifest themselves physically for children because they do not have the ability to put them into words.

Addictions:
This can include alcoholism, smoking, drugs (legal and illegal), pornography, comfort eating, sex etc. Alcohol and any other addictive substance like nicotine, or sex, increase the levels of the neurotransmitter dopamine. Dopamine is the pleasure chemical in the body that stimulates the reward system. Individuals who have a low self-esteem, a deep need to be loved and nurtured and are struggling with self-condemnation, guilt, shame or self-rejection usually have lowered serotonin levels. Serotonin is the neurotransmitter in the brain that is called the 'feel good' hormone, because it makes you feel good about yourself. Remember that your brain (hypothalamus) translates what goes on in your thoughts into a physical reaction. When your thoughts (mind) are filled with guilt, shame, self-rejection etc. the hypothalamus will lower the levels of serotonin. A lowering in serotonin levels cause you to feel bad about yourself and you reach out for something that will give you a sense of comfort such as a substance. As the drugs/alcohol are taken, dopamine (pleasure and reward chemical) is released and you begin to feel better about yourself. The problem is, however, that a person often feels guilty and/or ashamed afterwards because they know deep down that what they are doing is wrong and reinforces the low self-esteem, self-rejection and condemnation again – driving them to something that will make them feel better again. Thus, the cycle continues. A teen or adult survivor of childhood abuse will already have little self-worth, struggling with thoughts of guilt, shame and self-rejection which makes them easy 'targets' for addictions. Common triggers for addictions are peer pressure, introduction to illegal drugs or other substances or prescription

drugs (serotonin enhancers).

If there is alcohol addiction in the generational line, it results in a person being born with a defective or incomplete chemical in the brain due to the generational substance abuse. When this chemical comes into contact with alcohol, it 'pulls' the person towards alcohol and it only takes one drink to start the addiction cycle. Addicted parents should never encourage their young children to have a quick sip of beer or wine because it can change their lives in a very destructive way.

Sometimes a drug like cocaine is not as physically addictive but the body's response and the release of dopamine as a massive explosion creates a psychological and spiritual high and the person feels loved and complete. It is this feeling that drives them to more and more. The body, however, releases all the dopamine at once instead of regulating the release. This onetime massive release cannot be achieved for a second time because the body has released all that it had stored up and dopamine levels are depleted. It will take approximately two years for the body to restore the dopamine levels back to normal again. The person will never have that same high again and will look for something more in search to create the same sense of wellbeing and love. This can be extremely hazardous to your health and life threatening.

Unless you deal with the core issue of why you feel empty, unloved, unaccepted or unnurtured in the first place, you will always find a way to cope or feel better and in control. Substances causes you to live in a false reality, creating a false sense of comfort and control. Deep inside, you still have the inner conflict and a deep need for love and acceptance. Addictions are a cheap substitute for what Jesus Christ has done for us. It is not God's heart that you should be drunk, drugged or running from one false comfort to the next. In His embrace, you will find the ultimate love, comfort, nurture and sense of worth that you will never find anywhere else.

Eating disorders:
Bulimia and anorexia have different manifestations, but the same root cause which is a low self-esteem, self-hatred, disapproval/ rejection of self, condemnation and guilt. For this reason, survivors of childhood sexual abuse will be significantly more likely to display bulimic or anorexic behaviour. The children grow up rejecting, disliking and even hating their bodies because they are connected to the abuse, shame and defilement that come with it. There is desperation to look different or to look like somebody else or to have the 'perfect' body. Sadly, a person suffering from bulimia or anorexia has a distorted view of themselves and has no sense of acceptance, value or belonging.

Self-harm, self-injury:
This includes cutting, bashing their heads against the wall, burning themselves, pulling their hair out etc. People usually have depression, anxiety, personality disorders etc. and have self-harm as a secondary condition. People usually harm or injure themselves for the following reasons:

- As a child, going through the abuse, they were not allowed to connect with their emotions. They could not express the pain, confusion and rejection. When they, for example, cut or burn themselves, the physical pain they feel is an expression of the emotional pain and they can express pain this way.

- Physical injury results in a release of hormones, e.g. endorphins which affect the way they feel emotionally and act as a natural painkiller. It overrides (numbs) the deep and overwhelming emotional pain felt by survivors and becomes a coping mechanism and a false sense of comfort.

- Some people will cut on specific body parts, e.g. stomach or thighs, because of a negative association with those parts of their body.

Self-harm goes with a huge amount of guilt and shame, because the person knows deep down it is not the thing to do, but they feel they have to in order to get that release. They are also constantly anxious about the fact that other people might see the cutting marks or find out (it is always done in secret) and that leads to more shame and lowers their self-esteem. Parents or friends often do not know how to deal with it and react in a way that shows anxiety, anger and ignorance towards the self-harmer, instead of gaining more knowledge about the reasons behind it and how to help the person overcome this battle.

Suicidal thoughts and attempts:
Children who do not receive therapy reach a stage during adolescence and adulthood where the inner turmoil is too overwhelming. Constant anxiety and pressure from the outside world add to this feeling of oppression and hopelessness. Thoughts of terminating their life can seem like a reasonable way out.

No boundaries:
Children then become adults with no personal boundaries. Because of the fact that their personal boundaries have been ignored and overstepped when they could not stand up for themselves, they have no clue as to where they should draw the line physically, emotionally and spiritually. They grow up not knowing which type of touching is acceptable or even how to respect other people's personal space or needs. They may test rules about bedtime, homework or chores. School age children believe in rules. When something bad happens even if they obeyed, the rules then become oppositional and testy.

Propensity to revictimization in adulthood:
Often you will find that women who have been sexually abused as children will be attracted to men who are abusive. They have learned to dissociate from a young age when abuse was the norm, so they believe deep down that it is the way it is supposed to be. They have also learnt, from a very young age, to be submissive under people who intimidate and use them for what they desire.

Children also learn that they get attention or some sort of affection/comfort/love from the abuser and, as a confused, love-starved and often dissociated adult with a low self-esteem, they might be drawn to these perverted, abusive personalities.

Various types of depression, post-traumatic stress disorder, bipolar disorder, OCD etc.
Chronic activation of fear linked to the abuse results in anxiety disorders and depression in children, adolescents and adults, following events such as abuse/violence.

When you are diagnosed with depression or OCD, you are told that you have a chemical imbalance in your brain and need medication. That is very true, but not the whole truth. Remember that your brain is controlled by your mind (mind-body connection). What happens in your mind and emotions has a direct effect on the chemical/hormonal production, secretions and brain function. If you are in a constant state of fight or flight (fear and anxiety), there will be disorder in the body systems. The cause of the chemical imbalance should be dealt with and not just the chemical imbalance in itself. When you deal with the issues causing the imbalance, the body systems will come into order and function normally.

Multiple Personality Disorder (MPD) or Dissociative Identity Disorder (DID)
There is a disruption of identity characterized by two or more distinct personalities. This usually happens to victims of abuse who have endured and survived extreme sexual and/or physical abuse over a long period of time. It is often misdiagnosed as bipolar disorder or schizophrenia.

The person experiences different entities (fragmented person parts) manifesting. Some person parts maybe dormant for many years and only come out during adulthood or show themselves when the core person goes through counselling and prayer ministry through which they are triggered by emotions or memory. Sometimes a person part will be dominant and in control most of the time or for a few years until something triggers the other parts which will then come to the front and show themselves. People might also feel disconnected at some stages and have out of body experiences. I have ministered to people who said to me that for many years they felt like two or three different people living in one body, but could never understand, let alone explain what was happening on the inside. Many people will experience a strong drive to do something specific which is not something that they would morally or religiously consider doing, but they cannot help themselves – they just have to do it and in doing it, they feel disconnected and not part of the action/deed. Some person parts will be sexually very active, some might be bound in addictions, some might be very anxious and fearful or very angry and resentful. Some person parts will be little and childlike where others might be rebellious teenagers or strong, successful, in control adult personalities. Put all of these in one body, and you have disorder, distortion, disruption and destruction.

A person will suffer with amnesia (memory loss) which can range from small bits of the day to large chunks of their lives that are just missing and void. The amnesia is not only relevant to a trauma, but also to their everyday life. They might not remember saying or doing things during the day and find that there are certain time periods in the past wherein they cannot remember any detail of what happened to them or where they lived.

In satanic and occultic rituals, members of the cult/coven are traumatized through rape and violence in order to specifically cause fragmented person parts. These person parts are then used through mind control and demonic possession to fulfil specific functions or complete certain assignments. Satanic ritual abuse results in an individual having many, many person parts (even fifteen and more) with demonic entities attached to each one.

Although the demonic plays a huge role in multiple identity disorder (MPD), there is an extreme amount of brokenness and wounding in the human spirit and on a psychological level. A person with

MPD also deals with anxiety, fear, depression and insecurity and they do not only need deliverance and neither do they only need medication and a psychiatrist. They need long-term, intensive healing (spiritual, emotional and psychological) and deliverance from the demonic influence which attaches to each person part. Medication is not the answer, sanctification and healing is the answer to MPD. Although the person often longs for the chaos, confusion and pain to just go away, there is no quick fix in this regard because of our complex make-up and because God is not in the business of applying a band-aid. God knows every part of our being which needs healing and deliverance from the abuse and trauma and He alone can do it perfectly well when we submit and come into His presence.

Much of the harm caused to victims becomes apparent years after the abuse happens. Many disorders and diseases are a direct result of unresolved trauma. The body (sometimes over many years) has to cope with the internal wounding and stress which creates disorder in the body systems. Once the wounding and consequences thereof are dealt with, the body will return to function in a Godly order the way our Creator intended it to function.

What happens to the human spirit?

This is the most important part that needs healing, yet it is the part of a person which is rarely recognized because it is not acknowledged or understood. Medicine and science focus on the body and the mind/emotions and teach a person how to cope with everyday life in the midst of the inner turmoil. All this will not bring wholeness if the human spirit is shattered, imprisoned (in bondage) and defiled. The church usually supports science and will also encourage deliverance from demons, yet most spiritual leaders are not equipped or trained properly in the area of healing and deliverance. There is no teaching in the church about the demonic or the human spirit and yet it is the spiritual part of our being which connects with our Creator, Father God.

The terror and horror (lack of protection, rejection, violence, defilement, neglect and perversion) that survivors endure are often beyond what most people could ever believe. Conventional counselling methods will not lead these survivors of abuse to true freedom through Jesus Christ. As the child's free will was overridden and the child was never affirmed or acknowledged for who he/she is as a person, but for what he/she could offer, the child does not develop a healthy image of his/her value as a person. The child's personhood was never validated which not only causes a broken (shattered) and orphaned spirit, but also causes confusion and separation on a very deep level in the human spirit, such as:

- Confusion with regard to what pure love is;
- Confusion with regard to identity, sexuality, belonging and purpose;
- Separation from God as Father, Jesus Christ as Saviour and the Holy Spirit as Comforter, and
- Separation from self and from people around them.

The human spirit needs to be reconnected with God and, if there is severe fragmentation through dissociation (MPD/DID), connected to self. It is vital that the counsellor/minister engage with the human spirit (the person needing counselling and ministry). The human spirit needs to be legitimized, instructed and directed. The human spirit needs the sanctification, healing power, love and peace of the Father, through the work of the Holy Spirit, in order to bring wholeness. Renewing the mind is vital, but healing and cleansing of the human spirit is as vital for complete restoration, redemption and revival in a person's life.

When the spirit of man receives healing from abuse, the person becomes whole and the body and soul will flourish.

"A calm and undisturbed mind and heart are the life and health of the body" (Proverbs 14:30).

"A happy heart is good medicine and a cheerful mind works healing, but a broken spirit dries up the bones" (Proverbs 17:22).

"A glad heart makes a cheerful countenance, but by sorrow of heart the spirit is broken" (Proverbs 15:13).

"Why are you cast down, O my inner self? And why should you moan over me and be disquieted within me? Hope n God and wait expectantly for Him, for I shall yet praise Him, my Help and my God" (Psalm 42:5).

When a human being is mistreated or used as an object (abused), they are treated as less than a human being. These actions are not only actions against the person, but actions against God. How you treat the creation reflects on how you feel about the Creator.

Some food for thought:

Over the years, I have ministered to many people who were on psychiatric medication and I have never expected them to discontinue their medication because they come for counselling and ministry. Most of them, however, have been weaned off their medication (under the supervision of their psychologist/psychiatrist) as a result of the process of healing they chose to embrace. As said before, there is a time and place for medication and I cannot stress enough that a person should not quit taking their medication without proper medical supervision over a period of time.

I would like to give a brief overview of my personal opinion and some known facts of prescription medication as the only therapy for various types of depression, anxiety disorders and identity disorders:

1. In the case of life-threatening situations, medication can assist to stabilize a person, but it is not a long-term solution.

2. Biochemical changes in the brain are caused by emotions and thoughts – NOT by disease or mental illness. It is not the malfunctioning of brains which causes mental illness.

3. The mind, being an immaterial substance, cannot have a disease like the physical body does. Brains have disease but not minds. Fear, sadness and expression of deep emotional pain is not a disease but rather an expression of what is happening on a soul and spirit level. Wounded souls and broken hearts are real and the suffering thereof can be profoundly debilitating, but people should rather be taught how to express these emotions and how to work through pain – with God. The term 'mental illness' is often given as an explanation when confronted with these emotional behaviours and symptoms that are not understood on a spiritual level. Medication suppresses emotions and memories and numbs a person to what is really causing the disorder – bringing some relief, but no true healing. Taking medication which numbs you emotionally (just another way to dissociate) hinders healing as it is vital for the person to be in touch with their emotions in order to experience healing. Not only the 'negative' emotion is blocked, but the person will also find it hard to experience any joy, excitement and true peace. The impact of depression will diminish but at a price. Nothing is being healed – your spirit has been 'squashed' and your ability to feel has been compromised. You might seem more 'compliant' or in control but there is a separation from your 'self'. A blurred understanding and repressed memories caused by drugs hijacks the healing process as the person is not alert nor has a clear understanding or perception/ revelation. Psychiatric drugs do not heal. They block out the awareness of the deep brokenness and short-circuit one's spiritual growth.

4. Medication often teaches people to rely on science and not on the love, provision, protection and wholeness which

Jesus Christ died for. It becomes a crutch instead of turning to the Father and developing an intimate relationship with Him. Where does the church feature in this regard where wounded, fractured, abused beings need somebody to come alongside them on this extremely difficult and lonely journey to wholeness? A quick prayer or two or a two-hour counselling session is just not the answer.

5. Diagnoses are questionable. People are diagnosed according to a criteria list from the DSM (The Diagnostic and Statistical Manual of Mental Disorders). Diagnoses are based on the number of symptomatic occurrences in a given period of time. How does one quantify emotion and overwhelming fear and how often it should or should not occur to determine whether a person has a disorder or not? You might have several triggers to the anxiety, but might not be exposed to those triggers on a regular basis.

   Disorders often appear together like depression and anxiety. This, in my opinion, weakens the classification system because symptoms are not consistent and clearly distinguishable. Symptoms come and go depending upon surroundings and people. Different causes can lead to similar symptoms.

   People who are diagnosed with clinical depression might be suffering with similar symptoms from unresolved issues such as rape, repetitive loss, deprivation, emotional abuse etc. All these people will be lumped together under one classification (label), given the same drug regardless of the real cause and the fact that each person, their religious beliefs and their circumstances are different. Imagine a woman having been gang-raped at the age of 15, never dealt with it and now, at 29, she has anxiety and depression and tries to commit suicide. She is now diagnosed with clinical depression and given psychiatric drugs to cope with the overwhelming emotions and probable flashbacks of the traumatic incident years earlier instead of starting a journey of wholeness with the Father who created her.

6 Science or classification often results in labelling a person. These labels become their identity – they accept it and learn to live with it without the knowledge or expectation that there is hope for healing and wholeness. E.g. 'I have OCD'; 'I am Bipolar' and so on. Labels can not only put a person in bondage, but can also control a person's life. Sometimes the label becomes an excuse for a sinful lifestyle. Many times, I have heard the phrase, "Oh, excuse him, he is bipolar" or "she can't help it, she has a chemical imbalance". If the human spirit is connected to God, the person will have a sense of right and wrong and a person should take responsibility for his/her own sinful habits and behaviour, actions and reactions. Confession and repentance cannot be replaced by a couch or Cylift. Wholeness and living in a love relationship with the only True God cannot be replaced by Wellbutrin (Bupropion/Zyban). Science has reduced sanctification and what Jesus Christ has done on the cross. Unfortunately, the Church in general often partners with science in this regard because they do not know or understand how to deal with these people.

Psychiatric labels should not turn sin (one's own sin and the sin committed against you, or generational sin) into mental illness or a disease. Emotional suffering and pain are intensely spiritual issues. The Word of God and the life it offers provide the ultimate reference for the care and healing of a human being. What is 'normal' should be defined by the spiritual realities of the kingdom of God. Spiritual life involves things that the natural man, mostly, does not understand. Believers often see psychologists and/or psychiatrists who are non-believers who have no clue about the healing we find in God, through His Son, Jesus Christ and the power of His Holy Spirit. On the other hand, I have been in consultation with psychologists (if I accompany a patient) who are believers, but they stay true to what science teaches and separate the Word from their practice because that is what is expected from them.

7. Medication is marketed and sold through pharmaceutical companies who have to put their products through trial tests. These tests are usually done over a period of three months after which results are reported. What happens if you are on these drugs for more than three months? How safe and effective is it then? Mostly, only success results are reported. If there are twenty people on which a specific drug is tested and only four cases of the people respond positively, chances are that only those four tests will be reported as the success stories. Some of the websites for drugs will confirm that no long-term testing has 'yet' been done.

8. The issue of genetics is very much in question. For example, a disorder like schizophrenia cannot be genetic. This is why:

- More than sixty percent of schizophrenics have parents with no history of schizophrenia for many previous generations;

- Symptoms come and go depending on the person and their surroundings. If it was genetic in origin, the symptoms would be more predictable and regular;

- People diagnosed with schizophrenia are often very sensitive, with normal genes, but who have experienced some traumatic event or repetitive events, not dealt with it, thus resulting in outrage and overwhelming emotions which are not communicated properly;

- Data collected from studies done on schizophrenics and their families shows that the importance of nurture and understanding people's inner pain, confusion and trauma ensures that the person recovers and improves much more quickly – even without drugs;

- A two-year project done by Sorteria House showed that about 85 to 90 percent of newly diagnosed schizophrenics needing hospitalization recovered without conventional hospital treatment or drugs. If a safe, peaceful, loving environment can help people recover from schizophrenia, why consider genetics and drugs?

- Should you want to read more about the project of Sorteria House, you can find information at: https://en.wikipedia.org/wiki/Soteria_(psychiatric_treatment) or http://www.moshersoteria.com/ or https://beyondmeds.com/2011/02/22/soteria-2/

9. Psychiatric drugs come at a price. Beyond the financial implications, there are various harmful side effects – make sure that you are aware of these side effects. Here is a list of the most common prescription drugs and their generics. Below them, I will list the most common side effects of those drugs as reported by medical websites and pharmaceutical companies.

a) SSRI (Selective serotonin reuptake inhibitors) – to treat depression, OCD, panic disorder, post-traumatic stress disorder, bulimia, premenstrual dysphonic disorder and PMS:

Prozac (Fluoxetine / Rapiflux / Selfemra / Sarafem);
Citalopram (Celexa / Cilift);
Paroxetine (Paxil / Pexeva);
Sertraline (Zoloft);
Luvox (Fluvoxamine);
Escitalopram (Lexapro);
Vilazodone (Viibryd).

SSRI's are mood-altering and give one a false sense of peace.

SSRI's block the reabsorption (reuptake) of serotonin in the brain, making more serotonin available between the nerve cells. This creates a sense of wellbeing/peace. Serotonin is the chemical that was designed to make you feel good about yourself. Therefore, when serotonin levels are low, you feel terrible. The nerves try to compensate for this serotonin deficiency by increasing the number of receptors on the nerve cells (trying to absorb as much serotonin as possible, but there is not enough to absorb in the first place) and it is these excess receptors on the nerves which cause the symptoms of depression. Serotonin levels decrease when you have mindsets of self-rejection, a low self-esteem, guilt and shame. The lower the serotonin levels, the worse you feel. The worse you feel, the lower your serotonin levels drop – and the cycle repeats itself.

Summary of side effects:
Weight gain or weight loss; fever; heart palpitations; aggression; hostility; agitation; urges to self-harm; suicidal thoughts; pain/tenderness; swelling/bruising; unusual bleeding (nose, mouth, vagina, rectum, coughing up blood); vision changes (blurred vision, eye pain, eye swelling); kidney/liver dysfunction; lack of concentration; overactive reflexes; stiff, rigid muscles; memory problems; shallow breathing; dizziness; headaches; insomnia; seizure; anxiety; panic attacks; mentally/physically hyper; fainting; diarrhoea; nausea/vomiting.

b) Anti-Psychotics (Neuroleptics) – to treat psychotic conditions such as schizophrenia, bipolar disorder/manic depression in adults and children who are at least 13 years old. Also prescribed for irritability in autistic children who are 5 to 16 years old. It can sometimes be used together with antidepressants.

Zyprexa (Olanzapine / Zydis);
Risperidone (Risperdal);
Seroquel (Quetiapine);
Geodon (Ziprasidone).

Summary of side effects: Twitching (uncontrollable movements of eyes, lips, tongue, face, arms, legs); uncontrolled movements of head, face, mouth, neck; trouble speaking/swallowing; urinating less or not at all; high blood sugar; increased thirst; loss of appetite; dry skin; vomiting; sudden numbness; blurred/impaired vision; change in walking and balance; inability to sit still; loss of balance control; muscle trembling; jerking or stiffness; rapid weight gain; chest pain; laboured breathing; spasms of the eyelids; inability to move the eyes; bruising; loss of bladder control; bladder pain; loss of memory; lower back or side pain; nervousness; pain during sexual intercourse; pounding in ears; weakness of the arms or legs; headaches.

c) Central Nervous System Stimulants – to treat Depression, ADHD (Attention Deficit Hyperactivity Disorder), Obesity, Lethargy, Narcolepsy (a sleep disorder characterized by excessive sleepiness, sleep paralysis, hallucinations, and in some cases episodes of cataplexy [partial or total loss of muscle control, often triggered by a strong emotion such as laughter] and Postural Orthostatic Tachycardia (a condition in which a change from lying to standing causes an abnormally large increase in heart rate.[1] This occurs with symptoms that may include lightheadedness, trouble thinking, blurry vision, or weakness).

Ritalin and Concerta – These contain exactly the same active ingredient – Methylphenidate (a psychostimulant which works on the nerves in the prefrontal cortex of the brain where focus, logical thinking and decision-making take place. It binds to and blocks the dopamine and noradrenaline between the nerves. Methylphenidate also triggers the secretion of more dopamine and noradrenaline in the brain – both actions creating a sense of wellbeing and pleasure).

Prelu-2 (Phendimetrazine);
ProCentra (Dextroamphetamine);

Suprenza (Phentermine).

These stimulants are highly addictive.
Summary of side effects: Fast heartbeat; chest pain; fever; joint pain; skin rash or hives; black stools; blood in the urine or stools; blurred vision or change in vision; dry or flaking of the skin; muscle cramps; seizures; uncontrolled body movements; confusion; depression; suicidal thoughts; feeling like surroundings are not real; numbness of hands; seeing/hearing/feeling things that are not there; severe or sudden headache; mouth ulcers; unusual behaviour or weakness; agitation; anxiety; dizziness; anger; fear/panic; irritability; nausea/vomiting.

d) Other common antidepressants used to treat major depressive disorders –
Wellbutrin (Bupropion / Aplenzin / Buproban / Forfivo and Zyban). Zyban is also prescribed to help people to stop smoking.

Summary of side effects: Insomnia; nausea; pharyngitis; weight loss; constipation; dizziness; headache; abdominal pain; agitation; chest pain; migraine; skin rash; anxiety; confusion; hostility; hypertension; lack of concentration; heart palpitations; tinnitus; tremor; anorexia; abnormal dreams; fainting; false beliefs that cannot be changed by facts; seeing/hearing/feeling things that are not there; seizures; anger; aggression; being impulsive; high blood pressure; memory loss.

My own disorderly life:

I remember the day I desperately cried out to God and asked Him to heal me. After seeing two psychologists, a pastor, a reverent, a pastoral psychologist with a doctor's degree in both fields, gone for deliverance and still feeling that I was losing my mind, I realized that God is my only way out of the chaos I was experiencing. I made a conscious decision that I would not take any psychiatric medication if God would preserve my life and bring healing to my being.

A diagnosis, I must say, does bring some clarity and a sense of 'Ok, I know now what is wrong with me'. You can feel so overwhelmed and hopeless in not knowing why you are experiencing these things, but putting a name to it can bring some form of hope. The true hope comes when you can somehow, in the midst of all the insecurities, find trust in God to see you through the mess.

Through years of discipleship and ministry, I could make good decisions about medication and not taking on that label of MPD (DID). I knew deep inside that there was a better way. Was it easier to not take medication? I most definitely think not. I had nothing to dull the pain or to quiet the voices inside me. Some days it was hell. Other days it was better and I could cope. The days I had breakthroughs because of God's faithfulness, it was magnificent! Give and take, I would not exchange it for anything else. I not only found myself, but I found the love of my Heavenly Father.

Having MPD was intense in itself. I had a 4-year-old, a 6-year-old, an 11-year-old, a 17-year-old and a 20-year-old living inside me – each one with her own pain, confusion, distorted beliefs, anger, hate, rebellion, rejection, addictions, perversions and demons. Some of these person parts were more dominant than others, but they would switch roles as they wanted and when they were triggered by my surroundings and circumstances – very much without my conscious awareness. This was a result of generational abuse and incest in a masonic family line.

With that came:
- Memory loss (long- and short-term), dissociation, flashbacks;
- Anxiety, panic attacks, nightmares, suicidal tendencies;
- Fear of: pain/getting hurt, death, being alone, authority figures, punishment, rejection, failure, sexual assault, height and being in closed spaces;

- Depersonalization;
- Depression, exhaustion;
- Disease: IBS (irritable bowel syndrome), tumours/growths/cysts, cervical cancer, abnormal menstrual cycle, endometriosis, chronic migraine, regular unexplainable body aches/pains, stomach ulcer;
- Bedwetting and loss of bladder control as a child;
- Acne as a teenager;
- Chronic bacterial, viral or fungal infections;
- Shame, Guilt;
- Sexual dysfunction;
- Revictimization.

Unfortunately, there is no quick fix for this. It takes time. And more time. Often people turn to God for their healing instead of turning to Him for who He is. In discovering who He is, you experience a love that you have never thought existed. It is all about Him – for in Him you live and move and have your being (Acts 17:28). It is in His presence and in His embrace where wholeness begins – sin, disorder and disease cannot stand in the presence of our Mighty Healer. Just when you think you have seen the ultimate, you realize that there is so much more. He will never cease to amaze you. In the midst of the pain, He is there, even though it sometimes feels as if you will not see tomorrow. Take one day at a time – one battle at a time.

If you are on medication, don't feel judged or condemned. You can say 'yes' to His journey to wholeness while you are on medication and, as you experience His healing and redemption, you can be weaned off slowly but surely, under the supervision of your medical professional. I have worked with many people who were on psychiatric drugs for many years who have successfully been able to come off their medication over time.

There is hope...

PARTS *of Me*

He knows me so well
It is He who wove me together
In the dark womb of my mother
Creating a temple for my spirit to dwell
So intricately perfected
Filled with destiny and dreams
This is His Heart for me
The enemy came and perverted
Love and nurture, I cannot see
My spirit screams!
Shattered into pieces
My temple is in ruins
My spirit is disconnected
My soul is infected
Every part of me yearns
Surrender and struggle is the way
Journey to wholeness I choose
My life I lose
His Life I gain
Exchanging my pain
Becoming one in body, soul and spirit
Every part of me overflows with His Spirit
Covered in Love and cleansed by His Blood
Revival has come like a flood
I am whole!

Chapter 5

Saved by His Grace

I think at this point it is safe to say that we all believe that we are saved by grace, through the faith we have in Jesus Christ when we surrender our lives to Him and make Him alone Lord and Master of our life.

> *"For it is by free grace that you are saved through your faith. And this salvation is not of yourselves, but it is a gift of God"* (Ephesians 2:8).

> *"All are justified and made upright and in right standing with God, freely and gratuitously by His grace, through the redemption which is provided in Christ Jesus"* (Romans 3:24).

> *"We believe it is through the grace of our Lord Jesus that we are saved, just as they are"* (Acts 15:11).

> *"Made us alive with Christ even when we were dead in transgressions – it is by grace you have been saved"* (Ephesians 2:5).

Much is being taught about grace these days and there is some confusion around the true meaning of the above Scriptures. Many churches or denominations have various beliefs or perceptions on the topic of grace which can be truly freeing, or putting many people in bondage or leading many people astray.

Many believers are disheartened, hopeless and frustrated because they are taught that when you come to Christ in faith and receive His grace, you are truly free as the Word says:

> *"If the Son liberates you [makes you free men], then you are really and unquestionably free"* (John 8:36).

Yet that is not their experience. The Church is experiencing the same diseases and brokenness as unbelievers/the world. Whether Muslim, Hindu, Orthodox Jew or Christian, all suffer from depression, anxiety disorders or other physical diseases – Why? I believe that part of the reason for this lies in the fact that we do not fully comprehend the grace of the Father which we receive through faith in Jesus Christ and the provision for healing and freedom which lies in the finished work of the Cross.

> *"Let us stop going over the basic teachings about Christ again and again. Let us go on instead and become mature in our understanding. Surely we don't need to start again with the fundamental importance of repenting from evil deeds and placing our faith in God. You don't need further instruction about baptisms, the laying on of hands, the resurrection of the dead, and eternal judgment. And so, God willing, we will move forward to further understanding"* (Hebrews 6:1-3).

Let us look at the meaning of a few words/concepts and a number of Scriptures to get a clearer understanding of grace, salvation and sin.

When I talk about 'the Church', I do not mean a certain denomination or a building. I am talking about you and me; The people – believers in Christ Jesus.

The meaning of Grace:

- The free and unmerited favour of God, as manifested in the salvation of sinners and the bestowal of blessings.
- A divinely given talent or blessing.
- The condition or fact of being favoured by someone.

Synonyms: favour, approval, acceptance, esteem, regard, preferment, liking, support, goodwill, kindness.

Antonyms: disfavour, dislike, reject.

The word translated as 'grace' in the Bible is the Greek word *Charis* (G5485).

Charis means: The divine influence upon the heart and its reflection in the life;

Acceptable; Benefit; Favour; Gift; Joy; Liberality; Pleasure; Thanks; Worthy.

The meaning of being saved/salvation:

- Preservation or deliverance from harm, ruin, or loss.

Synonyms: lifeline, preservation, conservation.

In Christian belief: Deliverance from sin and its consequences, believed by Christians to be brought about by faith in Christ.

Synonyms: redemption, deliverance, saving help, reclamation.

Antonyms: damnation, downfall, destruction.

The word translated as 'saved' in the Bible is *'Sozo'* (G4982) meaning: to save, that is, deliver or protect (literally or figuratively)

– heal, preserve, save (self), do well, be (make) whole.

Salvation is the Greek word 'Soteria' (G4990) meaning: rescue or safety (physically or morally) – deliver, health, salvation, save, saving.

Thus, salvation or to be saved is NOT JUST coming to the Cross and accepting Jesus Christ as Saviour. When we say we are saved by grace through faith in Jesus Christ, it actually means: When we acknowledge our need for Jesus Christ and accept Him as our Saviour – making Him LORD (Master/Ruler) over our lives – we now can receive the grace (approval, favour, kindness, support, goodwill) of Father God – His divine influence upon our hearts which will reflect in our lives. It is this grace which empowers and supports us so that we can work out our salvation (our deliverance from bondage and sin, our healing and wholeness). That is what Jesus Christ has died for – making provision for our rescue, healing, safety and preservation (physically, morally and spiritually).

> *"So, my dear friends, just as you have always obeyed when I was with you, it is even more important that you obey now when I am away from you: keep working out your deliverance with fear and trembling, for God is the One working among your both the willing and the working for what pleases Him. Do everything without complaining or arguing, so that you may be blameless and pure children of God, without defect in the midst of a twisted and perverted generation, among whom you shine like stars in the sky, as you hold on to the Word of Life"* (Philippians 2:12-15).

The meaning of sin:

According to the dictionary, it is an immoral act considered to be a transgression against divine law.

Synonyms: immoral act, wrong, wrongdoing, act of evil/wickedness, transgression, crime, offence, misdeed, misdemeanour, error, lapse, to fall from grace.

In the Bible, we find that the word 'sin' is used many times and often translated incorrectly as there are various other root words, e.g. transgression, iniquity and trespass.

What is sin according to God?

- The word most commonly translated simply as 'sin', literally means 'to miss the mark' or 'to go astray' or 'by inference to forfeit'.

In Hebrew: châtâ (H2398)

Just as Jewish law, halakhah, provides the proper 'way' (or path) to live, sin involves straying from that path.

> *"And Moses said to the people, Fear not; for God has come to prove you, so that the [reverential] fear of Him may be before you, that you may not sin."* (Exodus 20:20).

> *"Your Word have I laid up in my heart, that I might not sin against You"* (Psalm 119:11).

> *"Who can say, I have made my heart clean, I am pure from my sin?"* (Proverbs 20:9).

In Greek: hamartano (G264)

> *"Jesus answered them, I assure you, most solemnly I tell you, Whoever commits and practises sin is the slave of sin"* (John 8:34).

> *"Blessed and happy and to be envied is the person of whose sin the Lord will take no account nor reckon it against him"* (Romans 4:8).

> *"For the wages which sin pays is death, but the free gift of*

God is eternal life through Jesus Christ our Lord" (Romans 6:23).

"Pay attention and always be on your guard. If your brother sins, solemnly tell him so and reprove him, and if he repents, forgive him" (Luke 17:3).

"When angry, do not sin" (Ephesians 4:26).

Trespass:

- To commit an offence against somebody else. To injure another person.

Translated as the word 'pasha' (H6586) – means a revolt, break away under just authority, rebellion or apostatize.

"So shall you say to Joseph: Forgive, I pray you now, the trespass of your brothers and their sin, for they did evil to you" (Genesis 50:17).

"I, even I, am He who blots out and cancels your transgressions, for My own sake, and I will not remember your sins" (Isaiah 43:25).

The same root word is used for both Scriptures.
Or
Mahal (H4604) – meaning treachery or falsehood.

"If anyone sins and commits a trespass against the Lord and deals falsely with his neighbour in a matter" (Leviticus 6:2).

"Did not Achan son of Zerah commit a trespass in the matter of taking accursed things and wrath fall on all the congregation of Israel?" (Joshua 22:20).

In Greek: paraptoma (G3900/G3895) – To fall away, deviation, to wilfully sin.

> "For if you forgive people their trespasses, your heavenly Father will also forgive you" (Matthew 6:14).

> "Even when we were dead by our own shortcomings and trespasses, He made us alive together in fellowship and in union with Christ" (Ephesians 2:5).

> "Israel has sinned; they have transgressed My covenant which I commanded them" (Joshua 7:11).

> "But they, like less-privileged men and like Adam, have transgressed the covenant; there have they dealt faithlessly and treacherously with Me" (Hosea 6:7).

> "The land and the earth also are defiled by their inhabitants, because they have transgressed the laws, disregarded the statutes, and broken the everlasting covenant" (Isaiah 24:5).

In Greek: parabasis (G3847) – to go contrary to, to violate a command.

> "And it was not Adam who was deceived, but the woman who was deceived and deluded and fell into transgression" (1 Timothy 2:14).

> "And for this cause He is the Mediator of the New Testament, that by means of death, for the redemption of the transgressions that were under the first testament, they which are called might receive the promise of eternal inheritance" (Hebrews 9:15).

Iniquity

And the word avon (H5771), or avah (H5753), means perverse (perversity), wickedness, to make crooked, a sin done out of moral failing – to continue with transgression.

> *"for I the LORD thy God am a jealous God, visiting the iniquity of the fathers upon the children unto the third and fourth generation of them that hate me"* (Exodus 20:5).

> *"Wash me thoroughly from my iniquity and guilt and cleanse me and make me wholly pure from my sin"* (Psalm 51:2).

> *"All we like sheep have gone astray, we have turned every one to his own way; and the Lord has made to light upon Him the guilt and iniquity of us all"* (Isaiah 53:6).

In Greek: Anomos (G459) means illegality, wickedness/evil, violation of the law, unrighteousness.

> *"Just so, you also outwardly seem to people to be just and upright but inside you are full of pretence and lawlessness and iniquity"* (Matthew 23:28).

> *"Who gave Himself for us, that He might redeem us from all iniquity, and purify unto Himself a peculiar people, zealous of good works"* (Titus 2:14).

> *"Thou hast loved righteousness, and hated iniquity; therefore God, even thy God, hath anointed thee with the oil of gladness above thy fellows"* (Hebrews 1:9).

Following the meaning of sin, we can see that there is a progression or moral decline involved. You start off by missing the mark; and we all do, for we are mere mortals. Judaism teaches that to sin is a part of life, since there is no perfect man.

Man is responsible for sin because he is endowed with free will ('behirah'); yet he is by nature frail and the tendency of the mind is to evil:

"For the imagination of man's heart is evil from his youth" (Genesis 8:21).

Therefore God in His mercy allows people to repent and be forgiven (provision Jesus Christ made through His death and resurrection). The problem comes in when we do not repent; whether we are ignorant or wilfully in rebellion, we will bear the consequences thereof. Unrepented sin leads to trespasses which leads to transgressions and, if we still do not turn to His regulations (Word), we will fall into iniquity. It is this iniquity which God clearly says in the Ten Commandments will have an effect on 'you and your generations to come'.

"Visiting the iniquity of the fathers upon the children unto the third and fourth generation of them that hate me" (Exodus 20:5).

Also read Exodus 34:7, Numbers 14:18, Psalm 109:14, Isaiah 65:6-7, Jeremiah 2:9, Jeremiah 32:18, Matthew 23:34-36 – the consequences for iniquity has generational implications.

The crime of sin has been dealt with at the Cross, but not the consequences thereof. In other words, when we make Jesus Christ LORD over our lives, we live eternally with Him – we do not die and go to hell. But the consequences of sin (brokenness, disease, barrenness, disorder etc.) is part of our deliverance, healing and walk into wholeness.

"And because you belong to Him, the power of the life-giving Spirit has freed you from the power of sin that leads to death. The law of Moses was unable to save us because of the weakness of our sinful nature. So God did what the law could not do. He sent His own Son in a body like the

bodies we sinners have. And in that body, God declared an end to sin's control over us by giving His Son as a sacrifice for our sins. He did this so that the just requirement of the law would be fully satisfied for us, who no longer follow our sinful nature but instead follow the Spirit. Those who are dominated by the sinful nature think about sinful things, but those who are controlled by the Holy Spirit think about things that please the Spirit. So letting your sinful nature control your mind leads to death. But letting the Spirit control your mind leads to life and peace. For the sinful nature is always hostile to God. It never did obey God's laws, and it never will." (Romans 8:2-7).

One of the reasons Christians/the Church are frustrated or hopeless is because we are sitting with a scenario of sinning saints (the Church) vs sinning unbelievers. Both are reaping the consequences of their own sin and the sin of their previous generations. We can be saved, but not sanctified. Sanctification begins by applying the law, regulations and precepts of God according to His Word. If we know His regulations, we know what is good for us and how to live as His children. When we miss the mark and sin, we repent because of the Blood of the Lamb.

Under both Old and New Covenants, we are saved by grace through faith. Salvation has never been accomplished in obeying the law. Under the Old Covenant we were saved by grace through faith in the sacrificial system which was a shadow and a type of Jesus' atonement under the New Covenant. Under the Old Covenant, it was the blood of goats and bulls and under the New Covenant it is the Blood of the Lamb – Jesus the Christ. The law does not save – it sanctifies us after salvation.

"For the life of the flesh is in the blood: and I have given it to you upon the altar to make an atonement for your souls: for it is the blood that maketh an atonement for the soul" (Leviticus 17:11).

"And he shall bring his trespass offering unto the LORD for his sin which he hath sinned, a female from the flock, a lamb or a kid of the goats, for a sin offering; and the priest shall make an atonement for him concerning his sin" (Leviticus 5:6).

"And he shall bring his trespass offering unto the LORD, a ram without blemish out of the flock, with thy estimation, for a trespass offering, unto the priest: And the priest shall make an atonement for him before the LORD: and it shall be forgiven him for any thing of all that he hath done in trespassing therein" (Leviticus 6:5-6).

Now you might say that that is Old Covenant Scripture, and I agree, but God does not change. He will not say one thing and then change it later. He is sovereign and holy in His ways and He does not lie.

"I am the LORD, and I do not change" (Malachi 3:6).

"So God has given both His promise and His oath. These two things are unchangeable because it is impossible for God to lie" (Hebrews 6:18).

"Whatever is good and perfect comes down to us from God our Father, who created all the lights in the heavens. He never changes or casts a shifting shadow" (James 1:17).

Jesus Christ said that if you have seen Him, you have seen the Father. He has the same character as the Father.

"Jesus Christ is the same yesterday, today, and forever" (Hebrews 13:8).

"God is not a man, so He does not lie. He is not human, so He does not change His mind" (Numbers 23:19).

Jesus Himself says the following:

"Make them holy by Your truth; teach them Your Word, which is truth. Just as You sent me into the world, I am sending them into the world. And I give Myself as a holy sacrifice for them so they can be made holy by Your truth" (John 17:17-19).

The Blood of Jesus the Christ cleanses us from our sin, trespass, transgression and iniquity. For this very reason we have to live a life of repentance.

"Under the old system, the blood of goats and bulls and the ashes of a young cow could cleanse people's bodies from ceremonial impurity. Just think how much more the Blood of Christ will purify our consciences from sinful deeds so that we can worship the living God. For by the power of the eternal Spirit, Christ offered Himself to God as a perfect sacrifice for our sins. That is why He is the One who mediates a new covenant between God and people so that all who are called can receive the eternal inheritance God has promised them. For Christ died to set them free from the penalty of the sins they had committed under that first covenant. Now when someone leaves a will, it is necessary to prove that the person who made it is dead. The will goes into effect only after the person's death. While the person who made it is still alive, the will cannot be put into effect. That is why even the first covenant was put into effect with the blood of an animal. In fact, according to the law of Moses, nearly everything was purified with blood. For without the shedding of blood, there is no forgiveness" (Hebrews 9:13-22).

The truth of the Word cleanses us and makes us holy – sanctification. The Word always leads us to repentance (dealing with sin and wounding) in order for us to be ready and set apart for our coming King – our Bridegroom.

"So that He might sanctify her, having cleansed her by the washing of water with the Word. That He might present the church to Himself in glorious splendour, without spot or wrinkle or any such things [that she might be holy and faultless" (Ephesians 5:26-27).

"And may the God of peace Himself sanctify you through and through [separate you from profane things, make you pure and wholly consecrated to God]; and may your spirit and soul and body be preserved, sound and complete [and found] blameless at the coming of our Lord Jesus Christ (the Messiah)" (1 Thessalonians 5:23).

Throughout the world today, we can see how the spirit of Balaam has crept into the Church – the very same spirit whom John warns us about in Revelation 2. This deceiving spirit has seduced the people of God for many generations, going back to Numbers 22-25 and 31.

Let us look at these Scriptures:

"Then to the angel of the assembly (church) in Pergamum write: These are the words of Him who has and wields the sharp two-edged sword: I know where you live – a place where Satan sits enthroned. [Yet] you are clinging to and holding fast My Name, and you did not deny My faith even in the days of Antipas, My witness, My faithful one, who was killed (martyred) in our midst – where Satan dwells. Nevertheless, I have a few things against you: you have some people there who are clinging to the teaching of Balaam, who taught Balak to set a trap and a stumbling block before the sons of Israel [to entice them] to eat food that had been sacrificed to idols and to practise lewdness [giving themselves up to sexual vice]. You also have some who in a similar way are clinging to the teaching of the Nicolaitans [those corrupters of the people] which thing I hate. Repent!" (Revelation 2:12-16).

First, God praises them about the fact that the Church is holding fast to His Name and they do not deny His Name in the midst of evil and destruction (a place where Satan dwells). Yet He rebukes them, because even though they are declaring His Name, they are holding on to the teachings of Balaam and the Nicolaitans. Now what are those teachings all about? Please read the abovementioned Scriptures in Numbers. In short, this is what transpired:

Balak was the King of Moab. Balaam was a false prophet (sorcerer) and the son of Beor. Balaam was widely known for his effective blessings and curses. Although he was not one of God's chosen people (messengers), he did acknowledge that Yahweh, the LORD, was indeed a powerful God. Sadly, he did not believe in God as the only true God. Balaam was a man ready to obey God's command as long as he could profit from it. Although he realized the awesome power of Israel's God, his heart was occupied with the wealth he could gain in Moab.

Balak wanted Balaam to curse Israel because Balak knew that Balaam's words always came to pass. Balak felt threatened and intimidated by the Israelites and he thought that he would be able to conquer them and drive them from the land if Balaam cursed them. But Balaam refused to curse Israel because he knew who their God was and that God Himself blessed them.

> *"But God told Balaam, Do not go with them. You are not to curse these people for they have been blessed!"* (Numbers 22:12).

Balak paid Balaam a bribe in order to try and control him. The riches he received were not encouraging enough to stand against the God of the Israelites. Balaam, however, did go on to teach the people of Moab how to seduce the Israelites.

> *"Why have you let all the women live? he demanded. These are the very ones who followed Balaam's advice and caused the people of Israel to rebel against the LORD"* (Numbers 31:15-16).

"While the Israelites were camped at Acacia Grove, some of the men defiled themselves by having sexual relations with local Moabite woman. These women invited them to attend sacrifices to their gods, so the Israelites feasted with them and worshiped the gods of Moab. In this way, Israel joined in the worship of Baal of Peor" (Numbers 25:1-3).

The main issue here is that Balaam's teaching says: As long as Israel has the blood sacrifice (blood for atonement of sins), they could come and play the harlot and feast with the Moabites. The Israelites were seduced and believed that it was all about the blood sacrifice – you do not have to follow the commandments if you have the blood atonement. Therefore, they partook in acts of immorality, fornication and idolatry. God was furious. Balaam was killed because of his counsel into seducing Israel. In a very subtle way, Balaam has instilled a false doctrine which not only the Israelites fell for back then, but we see it in the Church today.

The Nicolaitans were a group of professing Christians who introduced a false freedom or licentiousness – abusing Paul's gospel of grace which is identical to the doctrine of Balaam. People today are taught from the pulpit that it is all done at the Cross. You are forgiven, because Jesus has paid the ultimate price. You have the Blood sacrifice which makes atonement for sins. This is true, but they leave out the bit that says you have to repent and be sanctified and set apart. The Blood sacrifice made a way for us to live abundant lives but it is not an excuse to take part in acts of immorality, fornication or idolatry. In Revelation 2, which we read in the above section, God clearly says that He hates these teachings. Why? Firstly, because it is not truth and makes the work of the Cross cheap. Secondly, it sets a trap and a stumbling block before His children. This doctrine offers people a false freedom and a perverted mindset of what grace is about.

Grace empowers us to live a life of repentance and sanctification. It is not a reason to keep sinning and act as if we have arrived! God will not be mocked.

"Don't you realize that those who do wrong will not inherit the Kingdom of God? Don't fool yourselves. Those who indulge in sexual sin, or who worship idols, or commit adultery, or are male prostitutes, or practise homosexuality, or are thieves, or greedy people, or drunkards, or are abusive, or cheat people – none of these will inherit the Kingdom of God. Some of you were once like that. But you were cleansed; you were made holy; you were made right with God by calling on the Name of the Lord Jesus Christ and by the Spirit of our God" (1 Corinthians 6:9-11).

"Because we have these promises, dear friends, let us cleanse ourselves from everything that can defile our body or spirit. And let us work toward complete holiness because we fear God" (2 Corinthians 7:1).

"For the grace of God has been revealed, bringing salvation to all people. And we are instructed to turn from godless living and sinful pleasures. We should live in this evil world with wisdom, righteousness, and devotion to God, while we look forward with hope to that wonderful day when the glory of our great God and Saviour, Jesus Christ, will be revealed. He gave his life to free us from every kind of sin to cleanse us, and to make us His very own people, totally committed to doing good deeds. You must teach these things and encourage the believers to do them. You have the authority to correct them when necessary, so don't let anyone disregard what you say" (Titus 2:11-15).

"Don't be misled – you cannot mock the justice of God. You will always harvest what you plant. Those who live only to satisfy their own sinful nature will harvest decay and death from that sinful nature. But those who live to please the Spirit will harvest everlasting life from the Spirit" (Galatians 6:7-8).

The Word says that when Jesus has set us free, we are free indeed (John 8:36). This freedom or liberty means freedom from the control of the enemy and the bondage of sin which manifests only if we apply the Blood atonement in our lives. Repent and be sanctified by the truth of the Word of God. It does not mean that we are free to do what we want or what feels good. Our feelings are not necessarily in accordance with the truth. In fact, the truth can make us very uncomfortable so that we can get rid of all the 'stuff' we have been carrying for so long.

Issues are often 'candy coated' and people are not real about sin and in dealing with sin in love as Jesus does. Should we just keep staggering, be only 'half sane' and say, "We are going to Heaven"? This is not the gospel of Jesus Christ! Heaven doesn't need us; this world needs us now.

> "The law was brought in so that the trespass might increase. But where sin increased, grace increased all the more, so that just as sin reigned in death, so also grace might reign through righteousness to bring eternal life through Jesus Christ our Lord" (Romans 5:20-21).

> "What shall we say, then? Shall we go on sinning so that grace may increase? God forbid" (Romans 6:1-2).

When you come to Christ, you still sin every day. You still need to apply the Blood atonement every day. You need to deal with the consequences of the past immorality, fornication, lies, unforgiveness, guilt, shame, bitterness etc. His mercies are new every morning so that we can work out our salvation every day.

> "Now the Lord is the Spirit, and where the Spirit of the Lord is, there is liberty (emancipation from bondage, freedom). And all of us, as with unveiled face, [because we] continued to behold [in the Word of God] as in a mirror

the glory of the Lord, are constantly being transfigured into His very own image in ever increasing splendour and from one degree of glory to another; [for this comes] from the Lord [Who is] the Spirit" (2 Corinthians 3:17-18).

The Church is caught up between two worlds – their theology doesn't match the reality which they live in. They are bewitched with false security. You cannot give people false security and hope by quoting the right scriptures, when discipling and sanctification might be needed first. There has to be revelation of their spiritual state after which sanctification and reformation, from the inside out, follows.

We take so much time today to clean everything else around us – what about cleaning up spirit, soul and body? Or do we cling to the junk and expect God to heal us anyway, just because He loves us so much?

We cannot be calling bad good in the name of love or because we do not want to offend others. The above Scripture says that from glory to glory we are changed into His image – His character – His holiness. It is time to deal with the sin issues, pray for restoration and stop hiding behind grace and atonement.

> *"But He said to me, My grace is sufficient for you, for My power is made perfect in weakness. Therefore I will boast all the more gladly about my weaknesses, so that Christ's power may rest on me"* (2 Corinthians 12:9).

> *"Yet grace (God's unmerited favour) was given to each of us individually [not indiscriminately, but in different ways] in proportion to the measure of Christ's [rich and bounteous] gift"* (Ephesians 4:7).

God will give you His grace to carry you through.

There is so much falsehood and deception in the church today and yet the church is supposed to be a safe place for the broken and lost. Most people trust what the spiritual leaders teach and they do not know the Scriptures as they should. God warns us against these false teachers and false prophets.

> *"Beloved, believe not every spirit, but try the spirits whether they are of God: because many false prophets are gone out into the world"* (1 John 4:1).

> *"Now the Spirit speaketh expressly, that in the latter times some shall depart from the faith, giving heed to seducing spirits, and doctrines of devils. Speaking lies in hypocrisy; having their conscience seared with a hot iron"* (1 Timothy 4:1-2).

Now, Satan will not come at you with an absolute lie, because he knows that you will not fall into the trap. He will, however, work through spiritual leaders – using seducing spirits to lure you away from God's absolute truth and make you believe in doctrines of demons. Demons always lie and deceive – that is their nature. Their doctrines are not scripturally sound but contain only half of the truth. They lead you away from total loyalty and submission to Jesus Christ and the Word of God.

In 2 Peter 2, Paul explains that under the old covenant there were holy men who were moved by God's Spirit and spoke truth. Peter also warns in the next chapter that there were FALSE prophets (we can read about them in Jeremiah and Ezekiel) who had huge influence. Interestingly, Peter warns that there will be false prophets and teachers under the new covenant (in the last days). When we discern correctly, we will see that this is the truth in the Church today which confirms that this very warning of Peter is true and valid.

> *"But there were false prophets also among the people, even as there shall be false teachers among you, who privily shall bring in damnable heresies, even denying the*

Lord that bought them, and bring upon themselves swift destruction" (2 Peter 2:1).

The word 'heresies' means 'to choose or to take for oneself'. The word privily means 'to introduce secretively or without notice'. In other words, these false teachers will not reject all Scripture but choose how much Scripture they will believe and introduce it in such a way that people won't notice that it is false. These teachers are liberal and modernists – only preaching what is comfortable and acceptable to them. They do not deny entirely what Christianity should stand for, but they begin to appeal to intellectual honesty and sow doubt in the absolute truth. These teachings bring damnation to the Church. They are honest about what they believe, but they do not speak about the results of their denial in the absolute, complete truth which they choose not to believe. They speak ever so sweetly about love and grace till it drips like honey from their lips, but they are wolves in sheep's clothing.

> *"Beware of false prophets, which come to you in sheep's clothing, but inwardly they are ravening wolves"* (Matthew 7:15).

If there is no balance in their teachings on love, grace, sin, sanctification and holiness, there is something terribly wrong with that person's doctrine. God is a God of love and grace, but He is also holy and He does not change.

> *"Because it is written, Be ye holy; for I am holy"* (1 Peter 1:16).

If you deny sanctification, holiness, dying to yourself (flesh/sin) every day, forgiveness, the wrath of God, the reality of hell and judgement – what does that make Jesus Christ? There is no doubt that Jesus taught all these things and Jesus Christ was most definitely not deceived, neither was He a deceiver.

In Deuteronomy 13:1-5, God speaks against prophets performing signs and wonders or giving words which were not from the Holy Spirit – even if those words came to pass. Signs and wonders or prophetic words can come from other spirits too, not only from the Holy Spirit. We see that clearly when Moses went to Pharaoh – the magicians, who were using demonic power, copied the signs and wonders which Moses performed. This is not proof of a true teacher or prophet.

Sadly, these doctrines (Balaam/Nicolaitans) and the involvement in Eastern meditation/healing methods, the New Age teachings and the occult have given legal right for the Kundalini spirit to infiltrate and bewitch the Church. This spirit (also known as serpent power/ serpent energy in Eastern practices) presents itself as a 'false Jesus' and a 'false Holy Spirit' – focusing on love and grace and performing signs and wonders and miraculous healings. Christians often share experiences from encounters and visitations from this 'false Jesus', believing it is the true Jesus Christ (Yeshua).

It is this very same spirit that causes people to jerk, fall around, have uncontrollable laughter (not the same as being filled with the joy of the LORD), making animal noises and acting 'drunk in the spirit'. Being 'drunk in the spirit' is not Biblically correct. The term gets its name from the outpouring of the Holy Spirit on Pentecost, described in Acts 2. These men in the upper room were filled with the Holy Spirit and began to speak in different languages. When others heard this, they did not understand and marvelled about what they had heard. In verse 13, we read that there were some who mocked them and said that they were full of wine – just because they too did not understand what had happened. These men in the upper room did not fall around and act drunk or made animal sounds, the Word clearly says that they began to speak in different languages – which is a gift of the Holy Spirit.

The fruit of the Holy Spirit is love, joy, peace, patience, kindness, goodness, faithfulness, gentleness and self-control. According to 2 Timothy 1:7, we have a sound mind when our spirit is filled and empowered by the Holy Spirit.

Where the Kundalini manifests, there is no self-control, but rather disorder and often erupts into chaos. God (Yahweh) is not a God of chaos or confusion. If you look at the manifestations of Kundalini under the Hindu cultures and compare them to these manifestations of Christians who are 'filled with the anointing' or are 'drunk in the spirit', you will notice that they are exactly the same manifestations – very demonic in nature.

The idea that God would make people act drunk or laugh uncontrollably or make animal noises as a result of the Holy Spirit's anointing is directly opposed to the character of God. Nowhere in the Bible do you find anyone more filled with the Holy Spirit than Jesus Christ and not once did He act out of character or without control. Anointing, on the other hand, comes from the Father. It is not something that is passed on from person to person in these silly, airy-fairy meetings just because we feel we have the right to share His anointing. Anointing is a massive privilege and brings with it an even greater responsibility and accountability.

A false teacher/prophet in the church or a magician/diviner in the world will stand under the same judgement.

> *"For I am jealous for you with the jealousy of God Himself. I promised you as a pure bride to one husband – Christ. But I fear that somehow your pure and undivided devotion to Christ will be corrupted, just as Eve was deceived by the cunning ways of the serpent. You happily put up with whatever anyone tells you, even if they preach a different Jesus than the one we preach, or a different kind of spirit than the One you received, or a different kind of gospel than the one you believed"* (2 Corinthians 11:2-4).

Many churches are seeker friendly, people pleasing, social places of meeting where many are being deceived. That is not the gospel or the mandate! Jesus dealt with sin head-on, in love – bringing healing and deliverance to many. The mandate He gave us was, and still is, Matthew 28:19-20: "Go then and make disciples of all the nations, baptizing them into the Name of the Father and of the Son and of the Holy Spirit. Teaching them to observe (to watch and keep) everything that I have commanded you, and behold, I am with you all the days, to the very close and consummation of the age. Amen."

We first and foremost have to disciple people, teaching them about God and His kingdom – not just making sure that they have a 'wow' spiritual moment or a good experience. We have to teach them EVERYTHING which He has commanded us – not just what is soft on the ear and comforting. I have often seen that people repeat somebody else's prayer of salvation, get baptized and that is where it ends. Where is the discipling? Where is the teaching of the truth which Jesus has commanded us? Where is the lasting healing and deliverance?

If anyone denies the LORD Jesus Christ, His redemptive work on the Cross or teaches anything that undermines or denies any of these aspects of Scripture's truth, it is a damnable heresy.

Sin leads to disorder, brokenness and disease and has to be dealt with daily until the coming of our victorious King!

> *"He said, If you will listen carefully to the voice of the LORD your God and do what is right in His sight, obeying His commands and keeping all His decrees, then I will not make you suffer any of the diseases I sent on the Egyptians; for I am the LORD who heals you"* (Exodus 15:26)

> *"Confess your sins to each other and pray for each other so that you may be healed"* (James 5:16).

> *"But afterward Jesus found him in the Temple and told*

him, "Now you are well, so stop sinning, or something even worse may happen to you" (John 5:14).

"Because of Your anger, my whole body is sick; my health is broken because of my sins" (Psalm 38:3).

Obedience to His truth and confession of sin leads to spiritual cleansing, emotional and physical healing.

The Church is diseased, broken and defiled. She is not comfortable with pure, unconditional love. She has been stripped of her mantle. She has been blinded and lied to by the ruler of this world who works through those in authority who allow themselves to be deceived.

It is clear from the Word that there will be many who deceive and many who will be deceived in the latter days. Many wolves in sheep's clothing will come in His Name and teach false doctrine – the teachings of Balaam. Be alert! Do not be misled if it sounds good. Know what the Word of God says and you will be able to discern deceptive spirits working through false teachers and prophets.

"For certain men have crept in stealthily [gaining entrance secretly by a side door]. Their doom was predicted long ago, ungodly (impious, profane) persons who pervert the grace (the spiritual blessing and favour) of our God into lawlessness and wantonness and immorality, and disown and deny our sole Master and Lord, Jesus Christ (the Messiah, the Anointed One)" (Jude 4).

As teachers of the Word, we have a responsibility.

"Through Him we received grace and apostleship to call all the Gentiles to the obedience that comes from faith for His Name's sake" (Romans 1:5).

We are also accountable to God Himself for every word that comes from our mouths.

> *"And so each of us shall give an account of himself to God"* (Romans 14:12).

> *"So then, let us be looked upon as ministering servants of Christ and stewards (trustees) of the mysteries of God"* (1 Corinthians 4:1).

> *"If anyone does hurt to God's temple or corrupts it [with false doctrines] or destroys it, God will do hurt to him and bring him to the corruption of death and destroy him. For the temple of God is holy (sacred to Him) and that you are"* (1 Corinthians 3:17).

> *"And the servant of the Lord must not strive; but be gentle unto all men, apt to teach, patient, In meekness instructing those that oppose themselves; if God peradventure will give them repentance to the acknowledging of the truth; And that they may recover themselves out of the snare of the devil, who are taken captive by him at his will"* (2 Timothy 2:24-26).

Discipling and instruction bring revelation through the conviction of the Holy Spirit, leading to repentance and resulting in healing and deliverance from bondage. People need to change spiritually in order to ensure lasting change and recovery.

Unfortunately (for some people) we have to read the Word in context from Genesis right through to Revelation and believe that every verse is written for us. You will find nothing in the New Testament that is not mentioned or referred to in the Old Testament. The whole Bible is relevant, not only what we find comfortable or enjoyable.

> *"Every Scripture is God-breathed (given by His inspiration) and profitable for instruction, for reproof and conviction of sin, for correction of error and discipline in obedience, [and]*

for training in righteousness (in holy living, in conformity to God's will in thought, purpose, and action)" (2 Timothy 3:16).

"For the time will come when they will not endure sound doctrine; but after their own lusts shall they heap to themselves teachers, having itching ears; And they shall turn away their ears from the truth, and shall be turned unto fables" (2 Timothy 4:3-4).

Let us stop making a mockery of the grace of God and what Jesus Christ has done on the Cross for us! Do not take His grace and the power of the atonement for granted by teaching a watered-down gospel or by running after a sign or a word or a message that does not reflect the complete character of Almighty God and the complete truth of His Word.

God is testing your obedience. Fear God and do not go after falsehood. Judge every teacher of the Word and every prophet by their teaching and their relationship with God.

"As God's co-workers we urge you not to receive God's grace in vain" (2 Corinthians 6:1).

"Let us then approach God's throne of grace with confidence, so that we may receive mercy and find grace to help us in our time of need" (Hebrews 4:16).

"You were running the race nobly. Who has interfered (hindered and stopped you from) your heeding and following the truth? This [evil] persuasion is not from Him Who called you [Who invited you to freedom in Christ]" (Galatians 5:7-8).

Repent! (metanoeō) – Revelation 2; Matthew 4:17.

Change your thoughts, perceptions and understanding and return to His ways and the truth of His Word.

"Restore to me the joy of Your salvation and make me willing to obey You. Then I will teach Your ways to rebels, and they will return to you" (Psalm 51:12-13).

Chapter 6

Demonic Influence

"Stay alert! Watch out for your great enemy, the devil. He prowls around like a roaring lion, looking for someone to devour. Withstand him; be firm in faith [against his onset – rooted, established, strong, immovable, and determined]" (1 Peter 5:8-9).

Let me start off by saying that evil should not be feared. Just because we do not always understand something does not mean that we should fear it. God tells us in His Word to be wiser than a serpent and not to be ignorant of the devil's devices. Do not let an inferior kingdom control you. It is time to know your enemy and to know what he knows about you so that you can experience the abundant life you deserve.

I will give you a brief overview of how real, how structured and how organized the spiritual realm is. By no means, in discussing Satan and his inferior kingdom, do I give any glory to him, nor will I compare him as being equal or opposite to God. I do, however, want to show you that, although Satan orchestrates chaos, his kingdom operates in a very legalistic, authoritative and structured manner to succeed in their assignments.

THE AUTHORITY STRUCTURE OF TWO KINGDOMS:

There is a spiritual kingdom that submits to the will of God and a kingdom of darkness that opposes the will of God. These two kingdoms are not in any way equal and opposite, but there is a spiritual battle taking place which affects every person on this planet.

1. The Kingdom of God:
God is supreme and has sovereign power and authority over the created realms.
God is Spirit. God is also:
- Holy – He has never been touched by sin;
- Eternal – He has been before time and will always exist;
- Infinite – without limits except when He has limited Himself by His Word;
- Omnipresent – everywhere at once;
- Omniscient – all knowing;
- Omnipotent – all mighty;
- Truth – He never, ever lies;
- Just and Righteous – fair in all He does and He is always good;
- Life – He is Life and gives life;
- Unchangeable – James 1:17;
- Sovereign – absolute supreme Ruler. His sovereignty is in complete harmony with His other attributes. God never, ever steps out of character in any one of His attributes;
- Love – Unconditional love;
- Faithful – absolutely trustworthy;
- Merciful – beyond human comprehension;
- Provident – watches over and cares for His creation.

This Kingdom is ruled by unconditional, perfect love. God gives His children the gift of 'free will' through which we have the ability to choose to love and obey Him. When we are born again, we have authority over the enemy as we root and ground ourselves in His Son, Christ Jesus.

God created angels and only He has the authority to instruct them. Angels have different ranking and significance, e.g.

- Archangel – Michael (Jude 9, Daniël 10);
- Messenger angel – Gabriel (Daniël 8, Luke 1);
- Cherubim (Genesis 3, Ezekiel 10, Revelation 4);
- Seraphim (Isaiah 6);
- Other Angels (Revelation 5:11, 7:1, 8:6, 10:1 15:1).

They have different functions and job descriptions e.g.

- Worshipping God (Hebrews 1:6);
- To be in His presence (Matthew 18:10);
- Executing God's will (Psalm 103:20-21);
- Assisting and protecting believers (Hebrews 1:14, Psalm 91, 1 Kings 19:5, Matthew 4:11);
- Watching over the interest of churches/ministries (1 Timothy 5:21, Revelation 2, 3);
- Extraordinary acts (Acts 12:6-7);
- Releasing punishment on His enemies (Acts 12:23, 2 Samuel 24:16);
- Teach the law (Acts 7:53, Galatians 3:19, Hebrews 2:2).

2. The kingdom of darkness

Lucifer (the anointed cherub) is also a created being (Ezekiel 28:14-15).

He rebelled against God and was cast down to earth (Isaiah 14).

He rules this kingdom with fear, lies and deception.

His name, Satan, means 'the adversary of God' and all believers. (1 Chronicles 21:1, Matthew 4:10, Zechariah 3:1, 1 Peter 5:8).

His other names in the Word indicate his nature, e.g.

- Accuser of the brethren – Revelation 12:10;
- Liar and murderer (the father of lies) – John 8:44;
- Adversary, Devil, Roaring lion, Devourer – 1 Peter 5:8-9;
- Deceiver – Revelation 12:9, 2 Corinthians 11:3,14;
- Serpent/Dragon – Revelation 12:3-9;
- Tempter – Matthew 4:3;
- Thief – John 10:10.

Satan is not in any way equal to God. He is not a negative god, but a fallen angel. He is limited in location, knowledge, time and power (Job 1:6-7, Acts 19:15).

Fallen angels are not demons. Fallen angels are angels who fell from heaven with Lucifer (now called Satan) when God expelled them because of their pride and rebellion (Isaiah 14:12-17; Luke 10:18; Revelation 9:11; Jude verse 6).

What are demons and where do they come from?
They are not the spirits of dead people. Humans die once and their soul and spirit depart to either heaven or hell.

"And just as each person is destined to die once and after that comes judgment, so also Christ died once for all time as a sacrifice to take away the sins of many people" (Hebrews 9:27-28).

"But Abraham said to him, Son, remember that during your lifetime you had everything you wanted, and Lazarus had nothing. So now he is here being comforted, and you are in anguish. And besides, there is a great chasm separating us. No one can cross over to you from here, and no one can cross over to us from there" (Luke 16:25-26).

In Genesis 6, we read about the sons of God who had intercourse with the daughters of man. The sons of God were the fallen angels (Nephilim - Hebrew word 'Nef-eel' meaning:
- those who were cast down/to fall) who had sexual relations with the human women. This sexual act produced the giants of old. The giants were hybrids – half human, half fallen angel.

Demons are the spirits of these half-breeds who survived the flood and rose again through the line of Ham (Noah's son) and Nimrod (son of Ham).

Demons/unclean spirits are in the service of Satan and have the following characteristics:

- They have spiritual substance and need a body to act through – human or animal – Luke 10:19, Luke 8:33, Revelation 16:13;
- The demonic does not die when a person dies, but searches for a new host – transfers from one person to another – Numbers 19:11;
- They can hear/respond and they have knowledge – Luke 4:34, Mark 1:23-24;
- They have emotions – Matthew 8:29-31, James 2:19;
- They have a free will – Matthew 12:43-44, Mark 5:11-13;
- They attach themselves to objects, land and buildings – Acts 19:19, Leviticus 18:27, Genesis 4:10;
- They have a built-in fear system – Matthew 8:28;
- They walk – Matthew 12:43 (walk through dry places seeking rest, but finding none);
- They require worship and sacrifice (blood motivates them) – Leviticus 17:7, 2 Thessalonians 2:3-4, 1 Corinthians 10:20, Genesis 4:10;
- They recognize Jesus and believers with authority. – Mark 1:24, Acts 19:15, Mark 9:38;
- They drive and torment people – Mark 5:5;
- Give supernatural strength – Luke 8:29;
- They bring infirmity (Luke 13:11), slavery to fear (Romans 8:15), promote lying (2 Chronicles 18:22), jealousy (Numbers 5:14), and deception (1 Timothy 4:1);
- They are legalistic and know where they have rights – Ephesians 4:27, Acts 19:15;
- They have memory – Acts 19:15 – The demonic remembered Jesus and Paul and the authority they had;
- They know the scriptures and acknowledge the Trinity, the Cross and the Blood of Jesus.

They afflict, oppress, destroy, attack, do battle, cause trouble, take no food but hunger and thirst and they have no peace – the demonic battle against one another for authority. The demonic can work in groups and within an authority structure:

"For we wrestle not against flesh and blood, but against principalities, against powers, against the rulers of the darkness of this world, against spiritual wickedness in high places" (Ephesians 6:12 KJV).

"For our struggle is not against flesh and blood, but against the rulers, against the authorities, against the powers of this dark world and against the spiritual forces of evil in the heavenly realms" (Ephesians 6:12 NIV).

- Satan rules by fear/terror.

- Ruling spirits/Strongmen operate from the mid-heavens but can go back and forth between earth and heaven.

- Principalities control areas, e.g. countries, regions, cities, towns, neighbourhoods, churches, families (Daniel 10:13-20).

  When man is disobedient he gives the enemy spiritual authority over the ground, organisations or buildings that he occupies. (Leviticus 18:27).

- Earthbound demons/evil spirits and water spirits latch onto people to influence their lives and to bring destruction. The demonic does not attach itself to your spirit, because your spirit belongs to God. It influences your soul and lives in your body. For that reason, these spirits are cast out.

The following are examples of principalities:

Jezebel/Ahab, Pride, Anti-Christ, Mind Control, Witchcraft, Murder and Violence, Death and Hell (Hades), Mammon.

The following are examples of strongmen who focus on ways to keep people in bondage.

"How can one enter into a strong man's house, and spoil his

goods, except he first bind the strong man? And then he will spoil his house" (Matthew 12:29).

These strongmen are not cast out in the same manner as regular demons. They are:

1. Anti-Christ (denies Christ and Atonement, against Christ and His teachings, Heresies, Lawlessness, Humanism);
2. Bondage (fear, fear of death, addictions, compulsive sin);
3. Deaf & Dumb (dumb, mute, drowning, ear problems, mental illness, blindness, seizures, epilepsy);
4. Fear (fears, phobias, torment, nightmares, anxiety, lack of trust, doubt);
5. Infirmity (disease of body and spine, lame, impotence, asthma, oppression, cancer, weakness);
6. Jealousy (anger, rage, envy, hate);
7. Lies (gossip, slander, false prophecy, false teachers, accusations, deception);
8. Lust (lust of the flesh, lust of the eyes);
9. Perversion (filthy mind, sexual perversions, child abuse, abortion, doctrinal error, chronic worry);
10. Rebellion;
11. Witchcraft/Divination (fortune tellers, sorcerers, drugs, horoscopes, hypnosis, magic, rebellion, water witching etc.). Open the door to familiar spirits;
12. Whoredom (unfaithfulness, adultery, fornication, idolatry, prostitution, love of money).

Other common demons:
Demons work under the authority of strongmen and principalities and draw strength from them. They usually lure people into sin. E.g. Rejection, anger, anxiety, control, rage, familiar, Kundalini, addiction, pharmakeia, confusion, animal spirits, greed, zodiac signs, water spirits etc.

Examples from The Word:
Spirits of Infirmity – Luke 13:10-13;

Spirits of Fear – Romans 8:15; 2 Timothy 1:7;
Seducing Spirits – 1 Timothy 4:1;
Animalistic Spirits – Luke 10:18-19;
Death Spirits – Revelation 20:13-14;
Familiar/Guiding Spirits – Zechariah 10:2, Leviticus 19:31, 1 Samuel 28:7-8;
Antichrist Spirits – 1 John 4:3;
Jezebel Spirits – Isaiah 47, Revelation 2, Revelation 17;
Behavioural Spirits e.g. Lying – 2 Chronicles 18:22;
Unclean/defiling spirits – (look like frogs) Revelation 16:13-14;
Prostitution/Whoredom – Hosea 4:12;
Jealousy – Numbers 5:14;
Despair/heaviness – Isaiah 61:3;
Perversion – Isaiah 19:14.

> *All rulers, authorities and powers, for all time, are under the feet of Jesus Christ* – (Ephesians 1:2-23).

When we were in the world, the demonic controlled us but in Christ we have authority over them. Our weapons of warfare are not carnal, but mighty through God to pull down strongholds (2 Corinthians 10:4), silence the enemy (Psalm 8:2), bind the rulers/strongmen (Psalm 149:5-9, Matthew 18:18, Mark 3:27) and cast out demons (Matthew 10:8).

Can a Christian have a demon?

In the original Greek, the word 'daimonizomai' is used, which means 'to have a demon', 'to be held by a demon'. When we become believers and accept Jesus Christ, we become children of God and receive the Holy Spirit, but we can still be demonized (oppressed). Therefore, we can say that we can have the Holy Spirit and have a demon at the same time. Christians cannot be possessed.

When we are disobedient to God we give authority to Satan to operate in our lives.

"We know that we are children of God and that the world around us is under the control of the evil one" (1 John 5:19).

When Jesus Christ was on the earth, a huge part of His ministry involved dealing with demonic spirits in order to bring healing and freedom.

"And you know that God anointed Jesus of Nazareth with the Holy Spirit and with power. Then Jesus went around doing good and healing all who were oppressed by the devil, for God was with him" (Acts 10:38).

Peter himself was influenced:

"But Peter took him aside and began to reprimand him for saying such things. Heaven forbid, Lord, he said. This will never happen to you! Jesus turned to Peter and said, Get away from Me, Satan! You are a dangerous trap to Me. You are seeing things merely from a human point of view, not from God's" (Matthew 16:22-23).

Also, Ananias:

"Then Peter said, Ananias, why have you let Satan fill your heart? You lied to the Holy Spirit, and you kept some of the money for yourself" (Acts 5:3).

And Simon:

"Then Simon himself believed and was baptized. He began following Philip wherever he went and he was amazed by the signs and great miracles Philip performed. Let me have this power too, he exclaimed

Repent of your wickedness and pray to the Lord. Perhaps He will forgive your evil thoughts, for I can see that you are full of bitter jealousy and are held captive by sin" (See Acts 8:13-23).

Satan seeks to hold us in captivity to his authority. In Ephesians 2:2, Paul is talking to believers when he says: "You used to live in sin, just like the rest of the world, obeying the devil – the commander of the powers in the unseen world. He is the spirit at work in the hearts of those who refuse to obey God".

And in Galatians 4:9: *"So now that you know God, why do you want to go back again and become slaves once more to the weak and useless spiritual principles of this world?"*

When we participate with other people or in things that are outside of God's will, we become partakers with them of God's wrath.

> *"Don't be fooled by those who try to excuse these sins, for the anger of God will fall on all who disobey him. Don't participate in the things these people do. For once you were full of darkness, but now you have light from the Lord. So live as people of light. For this light within you produces only what is good and right and true. Carefully determine what pleases the Lord. Take no part in the worthless deeds of evil and darkness; instead, expose them"* (Ephesians 5:6-11).

How does the demonic get legal access to our lives?

Footholds can be established through our willing or unwilling participation in sin. This can happen due to a lack of Godly cover or knowledge.
Sin gives the enemy a foothold (topos: a space limited by occupancy) to work in our lives. (See Ephesians 4:26-27).

Sin is transgression against the instructions of God.
1 John 3:4:
(ASV) *"Every one that doeth sin doeth also lawlessness; and sin is lawlessness."*
(KJV) *"Whosoever committeth sin transgresseth also the law: for sin is the transgression of the law.""*

an'-om-os (law)
That is, (negatively) not subject to (the Jewish) law; (by implication

a Gentile), or (positively) wicked: without law, lawless, transgressor, unlawful, wicked.

The Jewish Law is the Torah (first 5 books of the Bible).
Sin needs recognition, confession and repentance before a loving Father (and sometimes other people).

Our willing or unwilling participation in sin creates a foothold. We usually sin due to a lack of knowledge, discipline or instruction. (See: Hosea 4:6; Isaiah 5:13; Proverbs 5:23; Ezekiel 44:23; 2 Corinthians 2:11; Isaiah 30:12-15; Isaiah 59:1-3.)

It can also be that we believe lies about God, ourselves and others. Walking in God's truth of who He is and who you are in Him will result in fulfilling God's purpose for your life and Godly, fruitful relationships with others. (See: John 8:44; 1 Timothy 4:1.)

Sin can be divided into four different categories:

a) Sin which you personally commit, e.g.

- *Addictions* (1 Corinthians 6:12; Titus 2:3; Habakkuk 2:16-17; 2 Corinthians 7:1)
- *Sexual sin, perversions, immorality* (Exodus. 20:14; Matthew.5:8; 1 Corinthians 6:13,18; Leviticus 20:10-26).
- *Idolatry; False religion* (Exodus 20:3-5; Psalm 115:4-8; 1 Corinthians 10:14:21; Jeremiah 44:8).
- *Occult involvement* (Deuteronomy 18:10-14; Isaiah 8:19-22; Leviticus 19:26,31; Leviticus 20:6-7; Isaiah 47:10:15).
- *Owning occult objects* (Joshua 6:18; Deuteronomy 7:25-26).
- *Self-rejection. You are a temple of the Holy Spirit* (2 Corinthians 6:16; Psalm 139:14).
- *Unforgiveness* (Matthew 5:23-24; Matthew 18:33-34).
- *Violence and murder (also abortion)* (Exodus 20:13); God gives life: (Matthew 5:21-22; Psalm 139:13).
- *Cursing with words* (Matthew 5:22; Psalm 34:11-14; Proverbs

6:17; Proverbs 12:18; Proverbs 18:21).
- *Control and manipulation* (2 Kings 9:22); God has given us the gift of freewill (John 6:66-67; Deuteronomy 30:19).
- *Submitting to healing methods and medicine outside of God's covering. Any form of healing that includes rituals, energy flow, altered (higher) consciousness, inner peace, life force flowing through meridians, chakras, chi or khi powers are rooted in other religions and will open the door to those spiritual influences in your life.* (Jeremiah 17:13; 1 Corinthians 10:20; Ephesians 4:17-18; Jeremiah 10:2-3a).

b) Sin which you are exposed to:

* Receiving abuse:
    Physical (Proverbs 4:14-17; Psalm 18:48);
    Verbal, emotional and mental (Proverbs 15:4; Psalm 55:21);
    Sexual (2 Samuel 13:19-20);
    Spiritual – misusing one's authority for self-gain.
* Being controlled by others (Matthew 19:5) – marriage.
* Unguarded contact with the dead. This opens you up for transference of spirits, e.g. familiar spirits, defilement or infirmity. The demonic needs a body (host) to operate in (Numbers 19:11).
* Receiving rejection, betrayal (Psalm 27:10; Psalm 22:9-10).
* Witchcraft/Cursing with words.

c) Being a victim or a witness of trauma

- Accidents or traumatic events which cause overwhelming fear or anxiety. The person feels insecure, vulnerable and uncovered/exposed, e.g. car accident, hijacking, burglary, rape, etc. (Romans 8:15; Philippians 4:6-7; Mark 6:50).

- Overwhelming loss and bereavement can lead to depression and oppression, e.g. the loss of a loved one (Luke 4:18).

d) Through your generational line:

Occult involvement, false religion, free masonry, fear and anxiety, iniquity, infirmity or disease.

Possible symptoms of demonization:
- Hereditary illness;
- Recurring body pain, heat/burning;
- Recurring illness without medical explanation;
- Disease;
- Torment/Nightmares;
- Drivenness, strife;
- Sexual sin, perversion;
- Bondage, e.g. addictions, abuse;
- Obsessive compulsive behaviour, emotional disturbance/ outbursts;
- Irrational fear/phobias, anxiety;
- Domination, control, manipulation, intimidation;
- Occult attraction;
- Death wishes, suicidal tendencies.

How demons manifest during deliverance (these manifestations are not always a guarantee of deliverance):
- Heat (sweat), trembling, shaking, palpitations;
- Lumps in the throat, deep breathing, sudden aches or pains/ headaches;
- Unnatural movements of hands or arms or legs, claw-like actions, pupils dilating, squints, convergence of eyeballs, slithering, sexual reactions;
- Demonic tongues, hissing, screaming, sudden violence, swearing, smells.

Demons may leave the person in the following ways:
- With no obvious or visible manifestations (person might say they feel 'lighter');
- Through the throat/mouth with deep breathing, yawning, burping, coughing, vomiting, choking;
- Through the eyes (crying, tears), ears (their ears feel 'open' –

almost like when you need to equalize and suddenly your ears feel open) or nose;

- Off the top of the head. They sometimes say it feels like something is lifted off their head.

At the Cross of Jesus, we are new creations, but there are still consequences of sin and the demonic from the past. Deliverance is a process of bringing Godly order in the place of disorder caused by Satan and the consequences of sin. A person exchanges the authority of the kingdom of darkness to the authority of the Kingdom of Light in his/her life. We live under the guidance and conviction of the Holy Spirit. It is Father God who reveals anything hidden or in darkness within us, if we ask Him. He knows the condition of our whole being. (Proverbs 20:27; Revelation 2:23; Jeremiah 17:10).

Be transparent, humble and test everything.

Sin needs confession, forgiveness and repentance. *Wounds* need healing and the *demonic* needs to be expelled. By following these principles, the demonic footholds (place of work) are taken away so that the demonic *has* to go. Deliverance and healing of body, soul and spirit go hand in hand and should not be separated.

> "…The reason the Son of God was made manifest was to undo (destroy, loosen, and dissolve) the works the devil has done" (1 John 3:8b).

What about POWER AND AUTHORITY?

In the beginning:
> God created the heavens and the earth. He is all powerful and the highest authority. (Genesis 1:1; Colossians 1:16; Matthew 24:30).

> Satan, who had authority, rebelled in heaven and lost his place of authority. (Genesis 1:26-28; Isaiah 14).

God created a human being (with body, soul and spirit) to have authority over the earth. (Genesis 1:26; Genesis 2:7).

Adam and Eve gave up their authority when they became disobedient to God and obeyed Satan in the Garden (Genesis 3:24; Romans 5:12; Ephesians 2:2; 1 John 5:19).

God's Redemption Plan:

God restored man's relationship and authority through a sinless Jesus. Jesus' freewill sacrifice brings restoration between man and God and disarms the authority of Satan (Genesis 3:15; Philippians 2:8; Luke 4:1-13; John 14:30; Colossians 2:14-15; Hebrews 2:14).

Jesus paid the penalty for sin by carrying man's iniquity (Isaiah 53:6; 1 Peter 2:24; Matthew 8:17).

The resurrection and ascension of Jesus was inevitable and vital (Matthew 20:18-19; Acts 2:24; Isaiah 25:8; Luke 24:46).

We have a free will to choose submission to the authority of Jesus Christ (Romans 10:9; Colossians 1:13).

In Jesus Christ, we are adopted into a new spiritual family and we are seated in heavenly places over Satan.

The Holy Spirit testifies with us and affirms our authority. We receive gifts and power (Acts 1:5-8; Galatians 5:22; 1 Corinthians 12:11).

Waging war for authority:

There is a war on contesting for inheritance until the second coming of Jesus Christ (Revelation 12:17; Revelation 13:1-2; 1 Peter 5:8; Revelation 12:10; Luke 22:31; Revelation 22:20).

In Christ, we have authority and power:

Authority: exousia (ex-oo-see'-ah): privilege, capacity, competency, delegated influence, jurisdiction, liberty.

Power: dunamis (doo'-nam-is): Force (literally or figuratively); specifically, miraculous power (usually by implication a miracle itself) - ability, abundance, meaning, might, strength.

> *"Then He called His twelve disciples together, and gave them power and authority over all devils, and to cure diseases"* (Luke 9:1 and Matthew 10:1).

> *"Behold, I give unto you power to tread on serpents and scorpions, and over all the power of the enemy: and nothing shall by any means hurt you"* (Luke 10:19).

> *"And I will give unto thee the keys of the kingdom of heaven: and whatsoever thou shalt bind on earth shall be bound in heaven: and whatsoever thou shalt loose on earth shall be loosed in heaven"* (Matthew 16:19).

> *"And He called unto Him the twelve, and began to send them forth by two and two; and gave them power over unclean spirits"* (Mark 6:7).

> *"And these signs shall follow them that believe; In My Name shall they cast out devils; they shall speak with new tongues; They shall take up serpents; and if they drink any deadly thing, it shall not hurt them; they shall lay hands on the sick, and they shall recover"* (Mark 16:17).

> *"Verily, verily, I say unto you, He that believeth on Me, the works that I do shall he do also; and greater works than these shall he do; because I go unto My Father"* (John 14:12).

Greater:
meizōn (mide'-zone)

Larger (literally or figuratively, specifically in age): elder, more.

With the background information you now have of the demonic, let us look at the role and dynamics of the demonic in the life of a person who has suffered childhood sexual abuse and generational abuse (incest).

Apart from the fact that the child will grow up with complex trauma, the generational line opens the child to demonic influence from the time of conception. The child is born under the consequences of the iniquity of the fathers, as it is written in *The Ten Commandments* (Exodus 20).

The receiving of sexual abuse at any given time during the child's formative years will then just reinforce and establish the many footholds and will activate the demons to influence the child. These demons will continue to operate in the child in order to derail him/her and cause destruction, disorder, disease and separation between the child (adult in later years) and God, separation between the child and other people as well as separation within the child. This separation takes place on a very deep spiritual, emotional and physical level.

Here are just some of the demonic influences and consequences which will be affecting the child:

- *The Anti-Christ*: This entity denies Christ, the work of the cross and the truth of the Word. It represents lawlessness and every evil thing. We can therefore say that generational sexual abuse is very satanic in nature as it reflects the anti-Christ spirit who rules in the generational line. It will make sure that the child grows up living in unbelief and anger towards God - wanting nothing to do with the gospel and Jesus Christ – rather blaming Jesus for the evil acts committed against him/her. The things of this world and what the world has to offer override the will of God, e.g. self-improvement, lack of submission, disobedience, greed, the desire for wealth and power, overindulgence, blasphemy etc.

- *Jezebel/Ahab:* Jezebel is only committed to herself, seducing people and ruling through spirits of lust, perversion, hatred of men, hatred of women, manipulation, control and intimidation. She loves child sacrifice and will ensure that the children in the generational line will submit to her sexual perversion and defilement, causing death and destruction on a spiritual and emotional level. The consequence is sexual sin, sexual confusion, sexual addictions/promiscuity, and ungodly control in adolescence and adulthood. The child who was controlled, manipulated and intimidated (Ahab spirit plays the victim) often becomes the one who controls, manipulates and intimidates (Jezebel) when she/he has the chance to rise up - seducing others to get exactly what she wants even if it means that she will bring harm to others. When it comes to sexual abuse, Jezebel will open the door to the spirit of infirmity to ensure sickness or disorder in the reproductive system.

- *Fear:* From a very young age, fear sets in. The child is controlled by fear to keep the secrets. Fear also causes constant anxiety which torments the child each day – expecting the worst and not certain when the 'next time' will be and how painful it will be. Years of repetition lead to fear on different levels, e.g. fear of getting physically hurt, fear that somebody will find out and what will happen to them if somebody does find out, fear of death, fear of people, fear of rejection, fear of punishment, nightmares, multiple phobias, doubt, lack of trust and immense insecurity.

- *Whoredom:* When being constantly used as an object of lust and promiscuity, the child believes that the body was created for that very purpose – to give oneself for the satisfaction of others and in return to receive some sort of affection or affirmation. The child (in his/her mind) was always good enough for what he/she does or did on a sexual level and not for who he/she is as an individual - perverted 'love' nicely packaged. This spirit drives the adolescent or adult into fornication, adultery, prostitution and worldliness. Girls will think nothing about showing off what they have to give and will flirt with anybody who will give them attention.

- *Witchcraft/Divination:* Cursing with words – the child will be cursed with many pronunciations, spells and hexes. Later in life, he/she will follow this learnt behaviour because of the deep anger, hate and resentment due to the injustice. It gives him/her a sense of 'being in control' of others.

The Word tells us that rebellion is as the sin of witchcraft (1 Samuel 15:23). The spirit of rebellion feeds an adolescent or young adult and they will take control and rise above the abuse. The mindset usually is 'I will look after myself' or 'Nobody will hurt me ever again' or 'I will not trust anybody to come close to me' or 'I will do it, I do not need anybody'. God and His Word is not an option because of the separation on a spiritual and emotional level. They will look for false security, guidance and comfort which opens the door for the spirit of addiction as well as familiar spirits and seducing spirits - leading them into fortune-telling, sorcery, zodiac signs and magic, meditation and new age practices.

- *Mind control:* This entity will keep the dissociation, the psychological split, the denial as well as the programming of the person parts in place. Mind control is often the culprit in mental disorders and keeps people in darkness.

- *Confusion:* Confusion sets in when somebody who is supposed to protect you, love you, nurture you and affirm your godly identity does exactly the opposite. Deep down in your spirit, you know that what is happening to you is very wrong, but you do not have any logical understanding about why this is happening. Abuse becomes the 'normal' and you have no idea that it actually is abuse. You just have to submit and be obedient. Over the years of abuse, you never learn your true purpose and identity. You have a perverted perception of what true love and protection is. You are confused about godly physical boundaries because your own boundaries were never established during the time of abuse. You never discover the liberty of saying 'no'. There is confusion over how a lady/gentleman should act and treat the opposite gender and also about what is normal in relationships and what is not meant to happen.

- *Heaviness:* Due to the constant rejection on a very deep level, the child has no sense of belonging or acceptance. The child develops a low self-esteem which later in life results in hopelessness, self-pity, depression, despair and grief. The spirit of heaviness keeps all these feelings in place, creating a perfect environment for suicidal thoughts to fester.

- *Lies:* That is the small little voice that can have such an enormous influence in a child's life. From conception, it will feed you lies about who you are and about who your God is. It reinforces the mindsets rooted in guilt and shame that says 'I am bad', 'It is my fault', 'I do not deserve a good life' etc. This lying spirit not only brings accusation, but reinforces falsehood - leading a person into religious bondage and false teachings and deeper deception.

- *Jealousy:* As a result of much anger, hate and resentment, the spirit of jealousy creeps in seeking revenge, causing strife and division and can ultimately lead a person to commit murder. Murder can happen on a physical level or on a soul level (1 John 3:15). Unforgiveness sets the stage for jealousy to become a stronghold.

- *Perversion:* God's intent has always been for sexual relations to manifest between husband and wife (within the marriage covenant) and to stay pure and holy – bringing man and wife together in unity. Perversion takes what God intended for good and contaminates it, making it defiled and perverted. The spirit of perversion not only creates a filthy mind, but also brings along incest, pornography, child abuse and homosexuality. All of the above causes a broken/crushed and defiled human spirit. (See Proverbs 15:4, Isaiah 19; Isaiah 5:20).

- *Infirmity:* This spirit operates in partnership with many other demons – it not only ensures sickness, but also weakness (physical and emotional), oppression, disorders and allergies.

- *Death:* The spirit of death (Death and Hades) brings exactly what the name says. It ensures death and destruction in the lives of people. This can be seen on an emotional and spiritual level, but can reach a point of physical death from a disease, murder or suicide. Ritual abuse or incest is a form of child sacrifice which slowly but surely causes a child to break on the inside and destroys his/her identity, purpose and reason for being alive.

- *Bondage:* This spirit ensures captivity to Satan. It will keep the victim bound in addictions, compulsive disorders and fear. You can get rid of all the other demons and strongmen, but if you do not deal with bondage, you will never break free completely.

Fragmented person parts are created as the trauma continues and the dissociation becomes more severe. The fragmentation process is a very brilliant survival mechanism the victim has in order to physically survive the violence and dehumanization. The victim can develop many person parts, each carrying the memory and pain of the abuse. The demonic will attach itself to every person part/identity in order to keep the separation and destruction in place. There can literally be hundreds of demons attached to each person part.

In Satanic ritual abuse, some of these person parts also carry instructions of specific mandates and duties which need to be acted out at specific times or places – as planned by those in control. These mind control techniques have very severe consequences and programming needs to be dealt with in a very precise manner as the very life of the core person depends on it. Apart from the above summary of the demonic influence connected to generational ritual sexual abuse, these victims of satanic ritual abuse also receive some more 'powerful' demons who are assigned to torment the victim when he/she does not act on instructions or does not comply with the rules those people in control have put into place. Science and the Church in general have the opinion that generational child sexual abuse/incest can be dealt with in one or all of the following manners:

a) The survivor is experiencing complex trauma (multiple disorders) and therefore needs medication and therapy. Therapy can take on many forms depending on the symptoms/manifestations the survivor is experiencing and the knowledge or preference of the clinician.

b) It is purely demonic and the survivor needs to forgive those who victimized, mistreated and violated him/her and must be delivered from these demonic entities.

Both these opinions are not the answer to true, lasting healing for the survivors of generational sexual abuse.

If you just treat a person with medication, you never deal with the extreme brokenness and mind-altering factors the person has to face each day. On the other hand, if you only try to deliver the person from an evil spirit, you can do immense harm to the core person as there are not only a few demons involved, but many are present and they all have a legal right and a job description. Each person part needs restoration, healing and deliverance. The pain (physical and emotional), sin and mind control from the repetitive traumatic experiences have to be dealt with systematically, on a very deep level, as God leads through His Holy Spirit.

It is a very complex process and can take many years for victims to recover fully. There is no tablet or shock therapy or quick-fix for generational sexual abuse as we were created as extremely complex beings. God, our Creator and Healer, brings healing and wholeness in ways which we cannot always comprehend. His ways are not our ways and His thoughts are not our thoughts. God knows ALL things, even the hidden things which we are not aware of.

> *"For My thoughts are not your thoughts, neither are your ways My ways, saith the LORD. For as the heavens are higher than the earth, so are My ways higher than your ways, and My thoughts than your thoughts"* (Isaiah 55:8-9).

> *"For who knows a person's thoughts except their own spirit within them? In the same way no one knows the thoughts of God except the Spirit of God"* (1 Corinthians 2:11).

> *"The spirit of man [that factor in human personality which proceeds immediately from God] is the lamp of the Lord, searching all his innermost parts"* (Proverbs 20:27).

Chapter 7

Journey to Wholeness

The journey to wholeness begins with surrender and submission.

- Surrendering to a Mighty Healer – He knows the very detail of every part of who you are.

  "It is the Spirit Who gives life [He is the Life-giver]; the flesh conveys no benefit whatever [there is no profit in it]. The words (truths) that I have been speaking to you are spirit and life" (John 6:63).

  "Humble yourselves [feeling very insignificant] in the presence of the Lord, and He will exalt you [He will lift you up and make your lives significant]" (James 4:10).

  "The sacrifice you desire is a broken spirit. You will not reject a broken and repentant heart, O God" (Psalm 51:17).

Realize that your healing is not more important than your relationship with God. He is your first love and the healing manifests as a result of your journey of intimacy with Him. Put your hope and trust in the Father and praise Him in the midst of what you feel or experience. When you feel lonely or depressed, meditate on God's Word, faithfulness and love.

"Why are you cast down, O my inner self? And why should you moan over me and be disquieted within me? Hope in God and wait expectantly for Him, for I shall yet praise Him, Who is the help of my countenance, and my God" (Psalm 42:11).

- Submit to godly authority – somebody accountable and trustworthy who understands your brokenness. Most importantly, choose somebody who is in a submissive, intimate and accountable relationship with Father God.

  "Confess your sins to each other and pray for each other so that you may be healed. The earnest prayer of a righteous person has great power and produces wonderful results" (James 5:16).

In Greek: *Dikaios* – equitable (fair and just in character or act); by implication innocent, holy.

  "Counsel in the heart of man is like water in a deep well, but a man of understanding draws it out" (Proverbs 20:5).

Also, choose somebody who has knowledge and understanding of how to help you while you are on medication. You cannot just stop your prescription medication because you feel it is the right thing to do. Your body chemistry has been altered and your body systems are dependent on the medication. You need to be weaned off it as you progress in the process of healing and restoration. Discontinuation of medication must be done under the supervision of your psychiatrist or medical doctor.

- Surrender to the journey. Embrace the way God chooses to bring healing in your life and lay down your own agendas, time limits and methods. In most cases it is not a quick fix and along the way you learn much about God and about yourself. Be willing to wait on God in prayer or silence.

"For we are God's [own] handiwork (His workmanship), recreated in Christ Jesus [born anew] that we may do those good works which God predestined (planned beforehand) for us [taking paths which He prepared ahead of time], that we should walk in them [living the good life which He prearranged and made ready for us to live]" (Ephesians 2:10).

"And I am convinced and sure of this very thing, that He who began a good work in you will continue until the day of Jesus Christ [right up to the time of His return], developing [that good work] and perfecting and bringing it to full completion in you" (Philippians 1:6).

Not your will, but the Father's will. This is not an easy one, especially if you have been doing things your own way for as long as you can remember. God knows the plans He has for you; you need to position yourself to receive what He has for you.

"For I know the thoughts and plans that I have for you, says the Lord, thoughts and plans for welfare and peace and not for evil, to give you hope in your final outcome" (Jeremiah 29:11).

"For My thoughts are not your thoughts, neither are your ways My ways, saith the LORD. For as the heavens are higher than the earth, so are My ways higher than your ways, and My thoughts than your thoughts" (Isaiah 55:8-9).

Vital things to consider in making decisions on your journey to wholeness:

1. Recognize that you need help.

2. Recognize that you desperately need God's intervention and that you cannot do this on your own anymore.

3. Recognize that thoughts in the mind are the fruit of the core beliefs in the human spirit. Only God the Healer can bring healing to the human spirit through the power of His Spirit.

"I the Lord search the mind, I try the heart, even to give to every man according to his ways, according to the fruit of his doings" (Jeremiah 17:10).

"God's love has been poured out in our hearts through the Holy Spirit" (Romans 5:5).

4. Recognize that these mindsets, thought patterns and attitudes which were produced over years must be taken captive because these things were never part of what God has for you. Often, they are very sinful and very destructive. This can be a process. It can take weeks or even months to break a habit. So, give God a little time to work on you as you draw closer to Him. As you walk out your healing, you will replace toxic thinking, bad behaviour and habits with godly ones. As you change your thinking, He will change you from the inside out. Renewing your mind is not something you do when you remember or when you have time for it – It is a vital part of every moment of every day. As you apply and appropriate the work Jesus Christ has done on the cross day by day, new long-term memory patterns of righteous behaviour will form. When issues come up, you will be tested. Your reactions will determine how much renewing has taken place.

"Don't copy the behaviour and customs of this world, but let God transform you into a new person by changing the way you think. Then you will learn to know God's will for you, which is good and pleasing and perfect. Don't think you are better than you really are. Be honest in your evaluation of yourselves, measuring yourselves by the faith God has given us" (Romans 12:2-3).

5. Be willing to be refined in His Fire.

"In [this] freedom Christ has made us free [and completely liberated us]; stand fast then, and do not be hampered and held ensnared and submit again to a yoke of slavery [which you have once put off]" (Galatians 5:1).

For the unbeliever, the fire of God is a devouring fire. For the believer, it is a refining fire. And He promises that the fire will not consume you. It is a safe place.

"When thou passest through the waters, I will be with thee; and through the rivers, they shall not overflow thee: when thou walkest through the fire, thou shalt not be burned; neither shall the flame kindle upon thee" (Isaiah 43:2).

"He burneth part thereof in the fire; with part thereof he eateth flesh; he roasteth roast, and is satisfied: yea, he warmeth himself, and saith, Aha, I am warm, I have seen the fire" (Isaiah 44:16).

6. Recognise what is not of God. Do an inventory of your life without guilt, shame or accusations.

"Solid food is for those who are mature, who through training have the skill to recognize the difference between right and wrong" (Hebrews 5:14).

"Let us go on instead and become mature in our understanding" (Hebrews 6:1).

7. Change is risky, especially for an insecure person. Be willing to change and to step outside of your 'comfort zone' no matter how uncomfortable it feels. Your world may not seem quite as safe and supportive as you want it to be. You may now find yourself on your own in your beliefs and have no one who understands the new things that you have just learned. God promises that He will never leave nor forsake you and that He always brings to completion that which He begins.

8. Allow God's truth to be the new absolute truth.

"I am the way, the truth and the life. No one can come to the Father except through Me. If you had really known Me, you would know who My Father is" (John 14:6-7).

Jesus Christ is Truth. He is the Word who brings all truth (John 1:1). As you learn the truth of the Word (not what is acceptable or comfortable) you get closer to the Father and you learn who He is and you discover your true identity. Fix your gaze on Him!

9. Take responsibility with God. Take responsibility for your choices. Adam and Eve didn't – fear, guilt and shame drove them away from the Father and the truth. Not making a choice is also a choice.

10. Accept reproof from God when He convicts you of something that is not in line with His Word. Sometimes He will use somebody else to show and teach you along the way. Remember that the Holy Spirit brings conviction. Guilt, shame and condemnation come from the enemy.

11. Confess sin, forgive people who have exposed you to things that are not of God and forgive those who have wronged you, even if you feel they don't deserve it. Forgiveness is not about them, it is all about you and your relationship with God.

"When I kept silence [before I confessed], my bones wasted away through my groaning all day long" (Psalm 32:3).

12. Renounce things like anger, gossip, lust, resentment, bitterness, guilt and shame, fear, addictions etc. Say it out loud because your words have power (power of life and death lies in the tongue) and you want your enemy to know that you are making good and Godly choices.

13. Stop making an idol of disease or brokenness. Sometimes somebody can be very ill and very dependent – needing much attention and care which is understandable. Sadly, I have seen in many instances how parents, in a very subtle way, draw strength from the encouragements, attention and pity they receive when a child has an 'incurable disease'. Despite the diagnoses of science/medicine and the suffering of the child, you as a parent can choose to align yourself with what God says about disease, drawing strength from Him alone. Reach out to people who can help in a positive way. Put your pride aside and deal with the issues that could have contributed to the disease and you won't feed the disease monster in your home – which can be extremely overwhelming and consuming. Often parents earnestly hope, pray and trust for healing but, at the same time, allow the disease to consume every area of their lives and the lives of people around them – it becomes their identity. Some parents desperately want their children healed, but they themselves are not prepared to be vulnerable and deal with their own issues (personal or generational) which could be a stumbling block in the child's healing process. Self-pity is your worst enemy and will only keep you connected to the past, hindering what God wants to do in the present. Self-pity keeps you from seeing the great future possibilities and only brings you and everyone around you down.

14. Guard your heart against unbelief, discouragement, despair and doubt.

"Keep and guard your heart will all vigilance and above all that you guard, for out of it flow the springs of life" (Proverbs 4:23).

15. Be careful of what you expose yourself to. Be very selective of movies, television programs, books and music. If you have issues with fear and anxiety or anger, do not expose yourself to things that reinforce or trigger those emotions. What you feed

will grow in your life. What you starve, will die.

"He who walks righteously and speaks uprightly, who despises gain from fraud and from oppression, who shakes his hand free from the taking of bribes, who stops his ears from hearing of bloodshed and shuts his eyes to avoid looking upon evil. Such a man will dwell on the heights; his place of defence will be the fortresses of rocks; his bread will be given him; water for him will be sure. Your eyes will see the King in His beauty; [your eyes] will behold a land of wide distances that stretches afar" (Isaiah 33:15-17).

16. Remove things from your life that bring temptation or that reinforce the very thing which you are dealing with, e.g. objects connected to the things you are confronting, magazines with pornography; remove alcohol or drugs from your home if you are dealing with addictions.

17. Sever ungodly ties with people who had a negative influence in your life – whether they are dead or still alive. Relationships where manipulation, intimidation, control or abuse is manifesting are not godly relationships. Stay away from clubs where you always hang-out. Make friends with people who will have a positive influence in your life and who do not represent/reinforce the issues you are dealing with. Sever ties with people who reinforce the 'label' of the disease or disorder in your life. These people will subconsciously keep you in your past, linked to the false identity you have partnered with and fuel the thought of 'this is who I am'. Take courage and make new friends, go to new places that will nurture and affirm who you really are.

18. Change your perspective of yourself. Gaze into the Father's mirror and behold the image which He is reflecting back at you. Read in His Word about who He says you are, for our Father does not lie. Once you view yourself differently, change will

happen in other areas of your life as well.

19. Resist your enemy. Be aware that he will not be happy with you when you turn your life around or when you go wholeheartedly after your creative purpose.

"So humble yourselves before God. Resist the devil; and he will flee from you. Come close to God, and God will come close to you" (James 4:7-8).

As you continuously resist the devil with all his lies and temptations, he will leave you. As you draw closer to Father God, He will draw closer to you. He will fight for you and protect you every step of the way.

20. Know that you are not alone on this journey of wholeness. Keep your focus on the Healer and you will overcome.

"Our inner selves wait [earnestly] for the Lord; He is our Help and our Shield" (Psalm 33:20).

Hold on to the promises of God and think about the positive things. Remember that everything that is good comes from Father God.

21. Always give thanks and praise to the God of your salvation!

Weapons of our warfare

"For when a strong man like Satan is fully armed and guards his palace, his possessions are safe – until someone even stronger attacks and overpowers him, strips him of his weapons, and carries off his belongings" (Luke 11:21-22).

In warfare, when the general surrenders, all the troops under his command automatically surrender with him. The same principle applies in spiritual warfare.

"So humble yourselves before God. Resist the devil, and he will flee from you. Come close to God, and God will come close to you. Wash your hands, you sinners; purify your hearts, for your loyalty is divided between God and the world. Humble yourselves before the Lord, and He will lift you up in honour" (James 4: 7-8,10).

"And they overcame (subdue, conquer, prevail, get the victory) him by the Blood (atoning Blood of Christ) of the Lamb, and by the word (spoken word) of their testimony (evidence given, record, report, witness)" (Revelation 12:11).

1. *The Blood of the Lamb: (Matthew 26:27; 1 Corinthians 10:16; 1 Corinthians 11:25)*
   - The cup of the covenant;
   - Defeated Satan;
   - Provision for forgiveness of sin (cleanses us from sin and the consequences thereof).

2. *The spoken Word: (Psalm 33:6; John 1:5; Proverbs 18:21; James 3:4-6; Ephesians 5:26)*
   - Jesus is the Word;
   - Defeated Satan;
   - Divides and separates Light and darkness, truth and lies/deception;
   - Cleanses us from incorrect mindsets, sickness and unbelief.

3. *Praise, worship, thanksgiving: (Romans 14:11; John 4:23-24; Psalm 149; Psalm 100)*
   - Exalting Jesus;
   - Worship Him in the fear of the Lord;
   - Giving thanks for what He has done;
   - God inhabits the praises of His people.

4. *Fast and pray: (Daniel 9; Matthew 17:21)*

- Breaking of strongholds;
- Submission and dependence on Him alone;
- Sacrifice the flesh.

"I have strength for all things in Christ Who empowers me [I am ready for anything and equal to anything through Him Who infuses inner strength into me; I am self-sufficient in Christ's sufficiency]" (Philippians 4:13).

Chapter 8

One New Man

"Just as a body, though one, has many parts, but all its many parts form one body, so it is with Christ. Even so the body is not made up of one part but of many. Now you are the body of Christ, and each one of you is a part of it" (1 Corinthians 12).

Our Creator has created us into different parts. He has created each part of our being to function in unity and harmony (to be whole), fulfilling one purpose and destiny according to His perfect plan. I trust that I have explained it in such a way through the chapters of this book, that you can see the magnificence of our creation.

The same goes for the Church – the body of Christ Jesus. It has always been our Father's heart for the Church – His children – to dwell in unity and function in harmony so that we can receive the abundant blessings He has for us. When I talk about blessings, I do not simply talk about money. I talk about health, wholeness and that we would walk in godly relations with others around us; that we, as a whole, can truly say, 'It is well with my soul'; that we would be like minded – having the mind of Christ; that we would live as the called-out Church – the Royal Priesthood – representing Him and serving Him; that the other nations would know us by the love we have for another. The unity and light which we reflect should draw the focus of the unbelievers to the one true God whom we adore.

If we, as individuals, are divided, broken and defiled, how can we fulfil our destiny as the bride of Christ? How can we say that we have the Mind of Christ if we, the Church, are fragmented and deceived? We need to get back to basics and hear what God says in His Word.

Paul challenges us to live worthy of the calling we have received – the awesome privilege of being called Christ's very own.

> *"Therefore I, a prisoner for serving the Lord, beg you to lead a life worthy of your calling, for you have been called by God. Always be humble and gentle. Be patient with each other, making allowance for each other's faults because of your love. Make every effort to keep yourselves united in the Spirit, binding yourselves together with peace. For there is one body and one Spirit, just as you have been called to one glorious hope for the future. There is one Lord, one faith, one baptism, and one God and Father, who is over all and in all and living through all. However, He has given each one of us a special gift through the generosity of Christ.*
>
> *Now these are the gifts Christ gave to the Church: the apostles, the prophets, the evangelists and the pastors and teachers. Their responsibility is to equip God's people to do His work and build up the Church, the body of Christ. This will continue until we all come to such unity in our faith and knowledge of God's Son that we will be mature in the Lord, measuring up to the full and complete standard of Christ. Then we will no longer be immature like children. We won't be tossed and blown about by every wind of new teaching. We will not be influenced when people try to trick us with lies so clever they sound like truth. Instead, we will speak the truth in love, growing in every way more and more like Christ, who is the head of His body, the Church. He makes the whole body fit together perfectly. As each part does its*

own special work, it helps the other parts grow, so that the whole body is healthy and growing and full of love.

With the Lord's authority I say this: Live no longer as the Gentiles do, for they are hopelessly confused. Their minds are full of darkness; they wander far from the life God gives because they have closed their minds and hardened their hearts against Him. They have no sense of shame. They live for lustful pleasure and eagerly practise every kind of impurity" (Ephesians 4).

"So we are Christ's ambassadors; God is making His appeal through us. We speak for Christ when we plead, Come back to God!" (2 Corinthians 5:20).

People should be able to see a difference between the Church (the Bride, Christ's ambassadors) and non-Christians, because of the way the Church lives. Going to church on a Sunday and celebrating Easter and Christmas does not make you the spotless Bride. The Bride is set apart and holy unto Him. Paul told the Ephesians to leave behind the old life of sin, since they were followers of Christ. Although we have a new nature, we do not automatically think all good thoughts and express all right attitudes when we become new people in Christ – it is a process. However, we are not to be driven by desire, impulse and lust after the things the world has to offer.

As you look back over last year, do you see a process of change for the better in your thoughts, attitudes and actions? How much brokenness, anger, rejection, licentiousness, pride and deception are still seeping through the cracks?

The spirit of the world (the lust of the eyes and the lust of the flesh) and the spirit of pride have lured the Church into a false sense of unity. As in the days of Biblical Babylon, denominations are building their own little kingdoms (their own tower of Babel) to see how high they can 'build'. It has become all about how much we achieve, how many evangelical trips we take to reach people and not who we are called to be; marketing, raising money, trying to fill the seats on a Sunday... Some are even advertising meetings as 'revival meetings' as if it is a commodity that could be produced at a scheduled time and place. Revival is not an event – it is a relationship!

We are not running the race well in order to receive the prize because we have lost sight of the goal.

> *"I press on towards the goal to win the prize..."* (Philippians 3:13-14).

The Church is taking some short cuts to get to the prize. However, Scripture warns us:

> *"Run in such a way as to get the prize... so that... [you] will not be disqualified"* (1 Corinthians 9:24-27).

God does not live in temples made by human hands – He has chosen hearts of flesh to make His glory known to the world.

Christ has come to give Himself for His bride in order to make her whole and to bring unity.

> *"Now may the God of peace make you holy in every way, and may your whole spirit and soul and body be kept blameless until our Lord Jesus Christ comes again"* (1 Thessalonians 5:23).

> *"He gave up His life for her to make her holy and clean, washed by the cleansing of God's Word. He did this to present her to Himself as a glorious church without a spot or wrinkle or any other blemish. Instead she will be holy and without fault"* (Ephesians 5:26-27).

> *"... to be strengthened and reinforced with mighty power in the inner man by the [Holy] Spirit [Himself indwelling*

*your innermost being and personality] ... that you may be
filled [through all your being] unto all the fullness of God
[may have the richest measure of the divine Presence, and
become a body wholly filled and flooded with God Himself]!"*
(Ephesians 3:16,19).

Spiritual awakening! – begins within your own human spirit, heart
and mind – one new man! Transformation begins from the inside
out and overflowing to the world – Revival! Every part of our being
healed, made whole and being strengthened daily by Him. Only
then can we rise up and shine as one new man – worshipping our
Father in spirit and in truth.

> *"But the time is coming – indeed it's here now – when true
> worshippers will worship the Father in spirit and in truth. The
> Father is looking for those who will worship him that way.
> For God is Spirit, so those who worship Him must worship
> in spirit and in truth"* (John 4:23-24).

The spirit Jesus talks about in this verse is your human spirit – the
core part of who you are – your innermost being and personality, not
your soul. You merely express what your spirit is saying. If your spirit
is crushed and defiled, you will find it difficult to worship a holy God
in truth and in complete surrender. Healing and sanctification brings
wholeness to the spirit – allowing it to rise up and to connect with
God on a much deeper level.

In days to come:

There will be a 'falling away' of the Church before the return of our Bridegroom.

> *"Let no one deceive or beguile you in any way, for that day
> will not come except the apostasy comes first [unless the
> predicted great falling away of those who have professed to
> be Christians has come]"* (2 Thessalonians 2:3).

There will be a separation between the wheat and the weed during the harvest season.

"Should we pull out the weeds? they asked. No, he replied, you will uproot the wheat if you do. Let both grow together until the harvest. Then I will tell the harvesters to sort out the weeds, tie them into bundles, and burn them, and to put the wheat in the barn" (Matthew 13:28-30).

There will be a separation between sheep and sheep – not just between sheep and goats.

"I will surely judge between the fat sheep and the scrawny sheep. For you fat sheep pushed and butted and crowded my sick and hungry flock until you scattered them to distant lands" (Ezekiel 34: 20).

There will also be judgement.

These things will be happening in the global Church about which God has forewarned us – we can be sure that God Himself, together with His Son, Jesus the Christ, will:

- Deal with the Shepherds and He will tend to the sheep.

Ezekiel is giving this message to Shepherds:

"What sorrow awaits you shepherds who feed yourselves instead of your flocks. Shouldn't shepherds feed their sheep? You drink the milk, wear the wool, and butcher the best animals but you let your flocks starve. You have not taken care of the weak. You have not tended the sick or bound up the injured. You have not gone looking for those who have wandered away and are lost. I will take away their right to feed the flock. I will rescue My flock from their mouths; the sheep will no longer be their prey. I will bandage

the injured and strengthen the weak. I will feed them, yes – feed them justice! I will rescue my flock and they will no longer be abused" *(Ezekiel 34).*

Zechariah says:

"Household gods give worthless advice, fortune-tellers predict only lies, and interpreters of dreams pronounce falsehoods that give no comfort. So my people are wandering like lost sheep; they are attacked because they have no shepherd. My anger burns against your shepherds, and I will punish these leaders. For the LORD of Heaven's Armies has arrived to look after Judah, His flock" (Zechariah 10:2-3).

"What sorrow awaits this worthless shepherd who abandons the flock! The sword will cut his arm and pierce his right eye. His arm will become useless, and his right eye completely blind" (Zechariah 11:17).

Isaiah prophesies:

"He will feed His flock like a shepherd. He will carry the lambs in His arms, holding them close to His heart. He will gently lead the mother sheep with their young" (Isaiah 40:11).

"He was amazed to see that no one intervened to help the oppressed. So he himself stepped in to save them with his strong arm, and his justice sustained him" (Isaiah 59:16).

• Gather His children:

"Hear the word of the Lord, O you nations, and declare it in the isles and coastlands far away, and say, He Who scattered Israel will gather him and will keep him as a shepherd keeps his flock" (Jeremiah 31:10).

- He will judge and make war against His enemies:

"For [the Lord] put on righteousness as a breastplate or coat of mail, and salvation as a helmet upon His head; He put on garments of vengeance for clothing and was clad with zeal [and furious divine jealousy] as a cloak. According as their deeds deserve so will He repay wrath to His adversaries, recompense to His enemies; on the foreign islands and coastlands He will make compensation. So [as the result of the Messiah's intervention] they shall [reverently] fear the Name of the Lord from the west, and His glory from the rising of the sun. When the enemy shall come in like a flood, the Spirit of the Lord will lift up a standard against him and put him to flight [for He will come like a rushing stream which the breath of the Lord drives]. He shall come as a Redeemer to Zion and to those in Jacob (Israel) who turn from transgression, says the Lord" (Isaiah 59:17-20).

"I am your enemy, O Mount Seir, and I will raise My fist against you to destroy you completely. I will demolish your cities and make you desolate, Then you will know that I am the LORD" (Ezekiel 35:3-4).

Mount Seir (also known as Edom) represents the people who oppose God; those who are proud, filled with anger, envy and hatred towards the people of God.

- Bring restoration:

"Then I will sprinkle clean water on you, and you will be clean. Your filth will be washed away, and you will no longer worship idols. And I will give you a new heart, and I will put a new spirit in you, I will take out your stony, stubborn heart and give you a tender, responsive heart. And I will put my Spirit in you so that you will follow my decrees and be careful to obey my regulations. And you will live in Israel,

the land I gave your ancestors long ago. You will be my people, and I will be your God. I will cleanse you of your filthy behaviour. I will give you good crops of grain, and I will send no more famines on the land. I will give you great harvests from your fruit trees and fields, and never again will the surrounding nations be able to scoff at your land for its famines. I will repopulate your cities and the ruins will be rebuilt. Then the surrounding nations that survive will know that I the LORD, have rebuilt the ruins and replanted the wasteland. For I, the LORD, have spoken, and I will do what I say" (Ezekiel 36).

• Breathe new life into the body:

"Dry bones, listen to the word of the LORD! This is what the Sovereign LORD says: Look! I am going to put breath into you and make you live again! I will put flesh and muscles on you and cover you with skin. I will put breath into you, and you will come to life. Then you will know that I am the LORD" (Ezekiel 37:5-6).

"When You give them Your breath, life is created, and You renew the face of the earth." (Psalm 104:30).

Our mighty, all-knowing, sovereign, Holy Father will not let His Word return void. His called- out ones – the Bride of His Son, Jesus the Christ – will arise – in unity, whole, adorned in her garments, without spot or wrinkle, ready for her Bridegroom.

Are you part of this 'one new man' rising up from the valley of destruction? Are you prepared, as the spotless bride of the Christ, to come out of your bridal chamber?

"Blow the trumpet in Zion. Let all the inhabitants of the land tremble, for the day of the Lord is coming; it is close at hand – Gather the people, sanctify the congregation; assemble the

elderly people, gather the children and the nursing infants; let the Bridegroom go forth from His chamber and the bride out of her closet. Let the priests, the ministers of the Lord, weep between the porch and the altar; and let them say, Have pity and spare Your people, O Lord, and give not Your heritage to reproach, that the [heathen] nations should rule over them or use a byword against them. Why should they say among the peoples, Where is their God? Then was the Lord jealous for His land and had pity on His people. Fear not, O land; be glad and rejoice, for the Lord has done great things!" (Joel 2).

"He who is able to hear, let him listen to and give heed to what the Spirit says to the churches" (Revelation 2).

Hear, Church, and be whole!

Testimonies

Over the years, God has brought many people across my path. Some I had the privilege of ministering to and others became friends and mentors. I now have the privilege of sharing the testimonies of just a few of these friends. These individuals, like myself, had to realize that there is so much more to human beings as a whole than what meets the eye. They too had to surrender to a holy God, submit to His way of healing, get rid of some false beliefs and expectations and trust Him above all.

Deric and Jacqui

Our story begins like many other couples. We got married in our twenties and enjoyed life together for a few years before we decided it would be a good time to start a family. After a year or so of trying to conceive and countless hormonal issues, we realized that there was something not quite right and we sought medical advice; all the while believing and trusting that God would come through for us.

We underwent numerous tests and were eventually told that, due to my endometriosis and some issues with my husband, IVF would be a good option for us. It was during this tumultuous journey that we met and established a relationship with Sylvia.

I clearly recall Sylvia approaching us one day in church, before we had even met, with a prophetic picture for us. She told us that she had seen an image of my womb and that it was red and glowing and healthy. This was a great encouragement considering the difficulties that we had been experiencing thus far. I wish I could say that our prayers were answered at this point and that our experience with infertility was over. However, it was rather the start of an incredibly difficult, but also incredibly enlightening journey.

Our prayer was always that God would receive the glory for any child that we were able to have. Thus, it was with mixed emotions that we embarked on our first round of IVF. All went well, although I produced only five eggs which, for a patient of only 31 years old, was considered a low number. The process went according to plan and, on day 5 of the process, two healthy embryos were implanted back. Then began an emotionally draining wait for the first pregnancy test a few days later. Sadly, the test came back negative and we were left feeling deflated and uncertain of our decision.

Sylvia remained a source of encouragement and a good friend through those dark days, often sending encouragements or kind messages. She was convinced that we would have children of our own and we held onto that hope.

A few months after the first IVF attempt, I underwent surgery to remove the endometriosis that had implanted on my ovaries. We felt positive that this would be the miracle we had hoped for; a natural conception, as this was what many doctors had told us. Sadly, nine months later, we were still childless and starting to feel a tinge of despair. What if this didn't work out for us? What if God wasn't going to give us our miracle?

As a result, we took matters into our own hands and decided to undergo a second round of IVF, still wanting the glory to be God's. The second cycle was fairly disastrous. They only harvested three eggs, none of which fertilized and hence the cycle was never completed. This devastated us and led us to begin to question all we were believing for in this area of our lives. The doctor we were seeing said that it was unlikely that we would conceive using my eggs and that we should consider using donor eggs. This was a devastating piece of information as donor eggs was not really something we would consider.

I cannot recall the exact timeline, but it was sometime after the second IVF attempt that we met with Sylvia to discuss some interesting perspectives that she had on the role of Freemasonry and ill health, both physical and emotional. After our discussion, my husband and I decided to go through a process of renouncing any hold that the involvement of both our great grandfathers had had with the Freemasons. We met with Sylvia and an elder at our church and began the process of verbally renouncing and 'undoing' the oaths that Freemasons take at various levels of the organization. I clearly recall reaching a stage in the process where I couldn't see the words on the page and felt dizzy and very out of sorts. It was later revealed that my great grandfather had been involved at that level of Freemasonry and that it was due to this that I had had this strange experience. The afternoon was concluded with an anointing with oil and encouragement.

Although we had been a little sceptical to begin with, neither of us can deny the change we felt after going through this 'cleansing' process. I felt less fearful, an emotion I had always carried around. Dealing with this spiritual aspect of our infertility is not something we fully understand, but it did shift something for both of us.

Ever hopeful that this would be the final step in our journey, we continued to believe for our family. We went up for prayer regularly at church during the process and would often receive encouragement and words of life spoken over us.

After another period of waiting and seeking God with no conception, we decided to attempt another IVF cycle. In this cycle, we changed doctors and felt that things were progressing well. The cycle only yielded three eggs, but the quality of the embryos from the process were so good that the doctor confidently told us to expect twins. This time things felt different. I felt that I was pregnant and was cautiously optimistic as the day of the pregnancy test got closer. Then, a few days before the test, all the symptoms I had been experiencing that led me to be hopeful disappeared. I was a nervous wreck and after a distraught phone call to the doctor's room, we did the test a few days early. To our utter amazement, the test was positive and I was told to continue with the hormonal support that I had been given after the embryo transfer. I was slightly nervous for the next test a week later, as I still had no symptoms.

However, we chose to believe it was all going to be okay. When I called for the results, I was gently told that the doctor wanted to speak to me; this was clearly not going to be good news. The test results sadly came back negative meaning that the pregnancy had been lost. This was a dark day for us and a time of real soul- searching. Throughout the rollercoaster ride we had found ourselves on, both of us had always had a sense of peace. After a few days of feeling very downcast, we both decided that it was completely in God's Hands and that we needed to take our hands off the steering wheel of our lives. This was December of 2010, three years after beginning this journey.

We decided to plan an overseas trip to family in Canada and try to take our minds off the infertility shadow that hung over us. Sylvia, ever faithful, continued to walk beside us through this ordeal and she suggested we take communion together fairly regularly and claim the promise of children. Throughout this process, Sylvia had a firm sense that we would have children and it was an incredible blessing to have her with us through the valleys. One night, late in February of 2011, I recall sitting on the couch in the TV room alone as my husband was on an overseas business trip. I felt a strange warmth in the area of my uterus. It was not painful at all, just warm and constant and it reminded me of the first word that Sylvia had given us in church about my womb.

Miraculously, on the 1st of March 2011 (the date is etched into memory forever), I took a pregnancy test as I was late, which never ever happened to me. The absolute shock and amazement that I felt when two lines appeared on the test was indescribable. A natural conception was what we had desired from the start and our prayers had been answered! My husband was in shock too and we felt too afraid to tell anyone for fear of something going wrong. As a result of all our problems conceiving, we decided not to tell anyone until we had reached the 12-week mark. We had every intention of telling Sylvia as soon as we had had our initial scan and seen a heartbeat. Incredibly, without having been told anything, Sylvia messaged me a few days after the pregnancy test and asked if I had any news to share with her. She knew before I even told her that we were pregnant as she had had a dream the night before about a baby boy. The gender of the baby was an interesting one for us as we believed our first child would be a girl, due to a prophetic word we had received that we would have a daughter and the name/word Zoe was mentioned. Needless to say, we were beyond delighted when we had a gender scan at 16 weeks and it confirmed that we were expecting a precious little boy.

Our story of faith and trusting God and choosing to deal with the spiritual complications of Freemasonry had a happy ending: 16 months after our son was born we welcomed a perfect little girl into the world. It is our firm belief that the natural conception and healthy pregnancies that I had are a miracle from God, but that we needed to take certain steps of obedience in order to deal with actions undertaken by previous generations in our families.

We have the great joy of being parents to a healthy 6-year-old son and 5-year-old daughter. We thank God daily and will never forget His goodness to us. It is through this ordeal that we came to know God on a deeper and more intimate level and we are forever grateful to Sylvia for the intimate role she played in this process.

Luke and Michelle

One of the hardest journeys of my life began when trying to start a family and, after a couple of years and three horrible miscarriages, I cried out to God and began to look for answers and solutions only He could bring.

A friend of mine introduced me to a kind, caring and wonderful lady who later became a friend. Her name is Sylvia. I truly believe that God used Sylvia and is still using her to intercede for His beloved through powerful prayer and intercession. Through many coffee dates and chats, I found that I was becoming more and more despondent until after about five months when Jesus' light began shining through the dark clouds and the pieces of the puzzle started coming together.

When I was 6 years old, I underwent a horrifying experience where I was molested and raped by my cousin for almost ten days whilst on a holiday in Cape Town. I did not tell my parents until I was 18 years old and l later suffered severe depression and anxiety. I underwent a year of counselling and antidepressants which thankfully helped at that time.

As I said, Jesus' light always shines through the cracks and He later revealed that my dad belonged to a Free Masonry Lodge where he probably didn't realize what he was involved in. Every time he went away over a weekend with this particular group, my mom suffered severe spasms in her lower back and felt very uneasy but at the time she didn't understand why she felt this way until the answers stared at us through my situation.

You see, whatever happens in the spiritual realm manifests itself in the physical, i.e. our bodies.

Parallel to our praying and meeting with Sylvia, my gynae thought that I had a protein S deficiency, which meant that my blood was clotting, but he required scientific evidence, so off I went and had many blood tests done. A couple of weeks later, my gynae phoned to say that he had conclusive evidence that I had a severe blood clotting disorder (usually hereditary and, when I asked about our family members, no one seemed to have the disorder).

It was about the end of November 2011 when my husband, Sylvia and two elders of our church began an extensive afternoon of prayer where I denounced things in my body, mind and spirit that shouldn't be there. It was a very emotional experience and, needless to say, during the following week I felt exhausted, overwhelmed and drained! However, I felt a peace that was tangible and surreal.

A week later, I was having coffee with a friend when I suddenly felt an urge to run to the bathroom. Quite disturbingly, I vomited up illuminous green sludge which I've never seen or heard of before. I felt like a spirit of deceit and lies came out through the physical, only for cleansing and new life to begin.

Through the chaos, stress, molestation and unhealthy spiritual realm I had been exposed to, my body presented characteristics of what spiritually was happening to me throughout my life.

Thankfully, God has blessed us with two gorgeous little boys who are full of fun and mischief!

My life is a testimony to His unfailing goodness, love, mercy and grace!

Thank you, Sylvia, for being obedient to His Spirit, helping those around you and most certainly using your anointed gift to bring forth truth and light to the world we live in.

Susan

The following testimony is of Susan whom I met at a healing ministry many years ago. Both Susan and I struggled with similar symptoms, yet the origin or root causes of our issues were quite different. Over a period of about five years, we laughed together and also shed many tears in pure brokenness and desperation together. She has been someone to whom I could just mention a word or a phrase and she would understand exactly what I meant and what I felt. When you are overwhelmed and it feels as though you are losing your mind, that is something you cherish. She is a beautiful daughter of our mighty God and I rejoice in the work God has done. I thank God for sending her on my path of wholeness and I thank her for sharing a brief description of her intense road to healing.

I have always thought that scarring and brokenness only happened when intentional and overt abuse has been your portion. To my surprise, I have learned that withholding God-given care, nurture and safety can be as damaging as intentional, deliberate abuse.

None of the withholding of care and nurture was intentional in my home of origin but the enemy had his eye on our family.

For me, a girl, the second child born after a brother, it started when my mother nearly miscarried me twice. My father was working far away from home for a few months. My mother telegraphed him and his reply was that he was not allowed to come home. The first and very strategic lie (from the enemy's point of view) that was told to me and by which I lived most of my life was, 'There are more important things and people than you.' This left me with little to no self-worth and an understanding of unimportance. Because my father, being the head, covering and chief protector of the family, was not coming, I thought I was not important enough for him to come when my life was threatened. It also robbed me of safety and predictability, not being sure that there would be someone to keep me safe when I felt threatened and unprotected. This formed the base from which I operated and also carried into my marriage. I did not expect to be first in my husband's life, nor did I expect him to be there for me, thus making very self-sufficient and independent. He would say to me, 'You don't need me', when in fact I craved nurture and protection but did not believe that I came first before his patients. He is a medical professional.

At the age of three, I lived with an aunt, whom I hardly knew, for six months while my father went overseas on business and my mother accompanied him. The lie that I had believed was now just reinforced as I had come to expect that my father was busy with important things but now my mother accompanied him and I was abandoned by both parents. This is the thinking of a three-year-old.

When I was about four years old, I was molested by a family member. In my veiled memory, I vaguely remember my brother being in the vicinity and wondered why he did not intervene; again, not being protected by someone older to keep me safe. By now, I did not expect to be protected and did not even consider telling anyone. I had accepted that this happens when there is no protection. This made me feel vulnerable and unsafe and, added to that, used.

When I was five, my mother had a baby, her second son. On day three, he started convulsing and was desperately ill for the first six months of his life. In that time, we were passed from home to home or lived with my mother in the hospital with the very ill baby. Again, my father was overseas with a sports team at the time of his death and burial. Having been abandoned by both mother and father, the 'abandonment lie' just tightened its grip. I now 'understood' that a desperately ill baby was more important than my needs and my life was insignificant and unimportant. I learned to be a quiet, well behaved, good little girl and took on the role of trying to be my mother's consoler, help and support.

Two years after my brother's death, my mother had another baby boy.

When I was ten, my oldest brother was in a very serious motorbike accident with multiple serious injuries and was hospitalized for four months. When he was released, he underwent intense occupational and physiotherapy for months, as he had lost the use of his right arm amongst other injuries. I again realized that being severely injured needed intense attention and my needs were insignificant and unimportant. My role as helper and carer was reinforced.

So, at the age of twelve, I understood and said to myself, "Okay, it's you and you alone. There is no one there for you. You have to go it alone. It is up to you now." A life of 'do-it-yourself' started and I worshipped at all the 'self' altars – self-reliance, self-sustaining etc. In my ignorance, I believed that I did not need anybody and I certainly did not need God.

Eventually, at the age of thirty-seven, I came to the end of myself and surrendered to my Lord and Saviour, Jesus Christ.

Only at the age of fifty-five did I land at a healing ministry and my healing journey started in earnest. On the last day of the 20-day Healing School, I discovered that I had what is called dissociative identity disorder.

This started a journey, for which I am eternally grateful, and for all the human help in the healing process; and so much more for my Saviour, Healer, Restorer, Comforter, Guide and Nurturer, without whom there can be no total healing nor full restoration - just maintenance.

I fractured while I was in the womb and at the ages of four and twelve. I gave each of the person parts a name and learned to see them as me, embrace them and love them.

The healing process was no easy ride and at times a very

disheartening process but oh, so worth it. It entailed visiting hurtful events with the guidance of the Holy Spirit, to see and repent of wrong thinking and attitudes and to forgive! I needed to allow the healing of the Holy Spirit into every situation and restoration of wayward emotions.

I needed to identify the different alters (person parts) and specifically their roles and functions and what caused them to form in the first place.

It was vitally important to understand what and who the triggers were that made me switch. So 'we' would have a conversation and anticipate trigger points and decide how to navigate through it. 'We' all needed to be on board and not have one alter switch on me and leave me acting like a twelve-year-old when I was in my fifties.

The healing process took about five years and another year later on.

I did not use medication as the issue never arose, not because of my doing, but by God's grace. I also believe I was at the thin edge of the wedge.

I am at a loss for words to describe my thankfulness for God's love, power and mostly His grace and longsuffering, without which I would be lost. Only His guidance and empowering can bring about healing with the help of people He used as His instruments.

To God Be The Glory
I am greatly honoured

Steve

I believe the most fearful of statements ever spoken in the Word relates to a sincere question asked of the Messiah: "Lord, Lord have I not healed the sick, raised the dead and cast out demons?" HIS heartfelt response being, "Get you away from me, I never knew you!" Plainly a response that raises mega concerns and leaves the enquirer more than somewhat unsettled or shaken, especially if the one asking is a healing evangelist. After an age of searching for a sensible yet feasible explanation, I read of the Seven Sons of Sceva. Those servants, who obviously being more than impressed by the Great Commission (and of what fame they could possibly achieve), opted to try and command and expel a powerful entity from a demon possessed man. This they tried without personal authority and to their downfall, it is biblically recorded, they were thoroughly beaten and ran off naked and bleeding. (add script) They had mistakenly surmised that, simply by using the Name of the Jesus Christ (The Messiah), whom they did not know, that it was sufficient to do the job. It was not! For plainly, the demonic know who has the authority of YESHUA! With me reading this very clear and outstanding statement, my previous Special Forces training instinctively clicked back into gear ... I had been fully trained to establish the strengths and detail of the enemy before engaging in combat. But it had been a lesson long forgotten whilst living in the comfort zone of the world. Know you well that although the demonic has some power, YOU as a believer have more than sufficient authority to cast out any demonic entity – they must leave their host without argument, for only when you know your GOD... will the demons obey!

Suffice to say, I gave my heart to Jesus Christ at midday on that Sabbath Saturday in October 1990. I was 46 years old at the time and, outside the normal age group to be born again, although many thought it to be a "flash in the pan", I never ever doubted that I had not been called to a greater "special forces" combat team, ever. I remember the exact moment of my conversion, the exact second of my infilling. I guess I had always understood the spiritual realm a little better than most, for I was an old hand at wrongdoing. I had cherished my dark knowledge serving the spirits and shadows of the world since a child. Being a born generational Freemason, I had family ties that went deeply into witchcraft, idolatry and druidism. I had also served 22 years in the ranks of Scottish, York Rite and Companion Templery. I had followed traditions, as had my forefathers before me and, although destined to be a dark adept, my life was falling apart at the seams. Albeit that I was in the fast lane, I was empty and dying.

Little had I known, my wife and children had been asking GOD for my life and HIS grace for my salvation.

By 23 February 1993, I was thoroughly born again. I had read the Bible from cover to cover seven times. Having done precious little but pray for the demon possessed, I learnt about demonically inspired illnesses – and about the amazing gift of discernment. During this three-year training period, I received a prophecy out of Habakkuk indicating that I would travel to the nations and be utterly surprised by what would transpire. From the time of this powerful prophecy, I have circumnavigated this globe some 26 times – walking in the signs and wonders of my Creator, ministering to kings and queens as well as unbelievers and have myself written several anti-occult books. I have seen the sick made well, the dead raised and countless demonically possessed souls set free. I am never unamazed at HIS grace and clearly add that I am not responsible for even one such miracle myself; the LORD has done it all. I have merely been a vessel that HE had used at that time. From the healing of cancer, restorative miracles and countless liberations from the occult.... all honour and praise to HIM alone.

However, in witnessing this, I acknowledge that I have truly learnt to "BELIEVE" totally without doubt and, most importantly, how to do just as HE asks, without pressure, without compromise, without embarrassment and, more often than not, completely without tact. I have learnt that 'no' is 'no' and 'yes' is 'yes', and any addition to this brings mixture....and I know HE accepts no mixture, and thus I have had to understand my GOD on a very personal level. I have lost friends, family, business and finances. Yet HE sustains me, HE is not just the Gentle Jesus that we make HIM out to be... HE can also get stern and this I have experienced on those few occasions when I have been at fault. I have learnt to hear and understand HIS voice, and HIS methodology; yet with this, I have never not felt HIS compassion and I have never seen HIM fail. HE is never subject to emotional extortion, and we are called to be like HIM in every respect, body, mind and Spirit.

Throughout all of HIS love and teachings, I have been schooled and shown that as HE is Triune, we are also...thus as we are body, soul and spirit, all proclamation for healing and deliverance must take place on three distinct levels; one cannot proclaim a healing to two out of three parts of a living being. As HE commanded, if you seek HIM with all of your HEART and all of your SPIRIT and all of your SOUL, HE will be found.

Even as you read this wonderful publication, know that my wife, Tina, has just days ago received her miracle and promise of life - she has been healed of 4th stage terminal lung and throat cancer. She opted to trust the Lord with HIS miracle healing than be subject to chemotherapy and radiation. Why not? Our Redeemer lives and today she is another proof of HIS prophetic promises. As JESUS said in the harmony of HIS Gospels...if all that has been done is put into print, there would be little space left for thanks. Blessings, health and joy to your body, soul and spirit.

❦

References

A More Excellent Way – Be In Health by Henry W Wright, –Pleasant Valley Publications 1999, 2000, 2001, 2002, 2003, 2004, 2005.

Healing through Deliverance by Peter Horrobin. – Sovereign World Ltd. 2007.

Healing Begins With Sanctification Of The Heart by Dr MK Strydom – Fourth Edition 2013.

Cure For The Common Life by Max Lucado – Thomas Nelson 2005.

The Body God Designed by Gregory L Jantz, (PhD) *with Ann McMurray* – Siloam 2007.

Switch On Your Brain by Dr Caroline Leaf; – 2013.

Strongman's His Name, What's His Game? New addition, *by Drs Jerry & Carol Robeson* – Shiloh Publishing House.

Snakes in the Temple by David Orton – Sovereign World Ltd. 2007.

Releasing Heaven On Earth by Alistair Petrie – Sovereign World Ltd 2000.

The Church In An Age Of Crisis by James Emery White – Baker Books 2012.

Purging Your House, Pruning Your Family Tree by Perry Stone – Charisma House 2011.

The Calvary Road by Roy Hession – OM Books 2013.

Pills For The Soul by Dieter K. Mulitze PhD – Sovereign World Ltd 2005, 2008.

Christian Counselling by Gary R. Collins, PhD, 2007.

Webpage references:
    www.madinamerica.com
    www.healyprozac.com
    www.socialudit.uk.org
    www.secasa.com.au
    www.drugs.com
    www.webmed.com
    www.emedicinehealth.com
    www.mayoclinic.org
    www.health24.com